AUG 12 1993

THE PRACTICAL GUIDE TO CANADIAN LEGAL RESEARCH

Jacqueline R. Castel, B.A., LL.B.
of the Ontario Bar

Omeela K. Latchman, B.Sc., LL.B.
of the Ontario Bar

CARSWELL
Thomson Professional Publishing

This publication is designed to provide accurate and authoritative information. It is sold with the understanding that the publisher and authors are not engaged in rendering legal, accounting or other professional advice. If legal advice or other expert assistance is required, the services of a competent professional should be sought. The analysis contained herein should in no way be construed as being either official or unofficial policy of any governmental body.

Canadian Cataloguing in Publication Data

Castel, Jacqueline R., 1965-
   The practical guide to Canadian legal research

Includes bibliographical references and index.
ISBN 0-459-55178-7

1. Legal research — Canada.   I. Latchman,
Omeela K., 1965-   . II. Title.

KE250.C3 1993   340'.072071   C93-093603-5
KF240.C3 1993

Front cover illustration "Ariadne and the Labyrinth" by Sheila P. Latchman.
© 1993 Jacqueline R. Castel and Omeela K. Latchman.

CARSWELL
Thomson Professional Publishing

One Corporate Plaza, 2075 Kennedy Road, Scarborough, Ontario M1T 3V4
Customer Service:
Toronto 1-416-609-3800
Elsewhere in Canada/U.S. 1-800-387-5164
Fax 1-416-298-5094

We dedicate this book to our parents,
André Castel and Helene Moussa,
and
Kumar Latchman and Sheila Latchman

Foreword

Familiarity with the law library is essential for all law students and lawyers. Yet despite the importance of the tools and techniques of legal research, it is difficult to point to a reliable and "user-friendly" book on the subject. *The Practical Guide to Canadian Legal Research* fills this significant gap in the literature.

This book provides a systematic approach to legal research in the common law system. Not only are research tools described in a clear and comprehensive manner, the authors go beyond description and explain when and how it is useful to use the various tools in the research process. Their aim is pragmatic and their focus is strategic. Vague generalities are avoided and one finds a strong emphasis upon problem solving. The result is a product that can be used as an effective tool by the reader who requires immediate access to legal materials.

The book begins by describing the basic mechanics of the common law system and provides a flow chart for prioritizing the law. This flow chart equips the reader with a logical and coherent road map of available legal materials. It will assist the researcher in finding order in the mass of legal materials and in coping with the deluge of information research often produces. It will not only point the user in the right direction but will also prevent the reader from getting lost in the detail and failing to appreciate the broader perspective.

The book centres around a checklist of the principal tools for Canadian legal research. This checklist allows the user to proceed in an orderly and organized fashion, starting with secondary sources, and then proceeding to primary sources. The authors explain both the "how" and "why" at each stage, and provide extensive cross-referencing to reinforce the interconnectedness of the various stages and tools of legal research.

The book offers a comprehensive catalogue and guide to Canadian law library research materials, including texts and treatises, periodicals and conference materials, looseleaf services, digests, abridgments, access to unreported decisions, dictionaries, and as well treats English and American legal materials.

Non-traditional research tools are described and their use is encouraged. Again, the approach is pragmatic. The authors discuss, for example, how press reports can be used to provide a wide array of useful information on matters such as background of clients and opponents and details of settlements, information not available from case reports and legal texts.

Jacqueline Castel and Omeela Latchman, recent graduates of the Faculty of Law, University of Toronto, are to be commended for writing this valuable book on Canadian legal research. It is a welcome addition to the sparse literature on the subject. It provides those embarking upon legal research with a systematic and reliable guide, and even experienced researchers will derive benefit from the pages which follow.

Robert J. Sharpe
Dean, Faculty of Law,
University of Toronto

Acknowledgments

We are grateful for the kind assistance of: Danny Lang and Alan Treleaven for their thoughtful comments on a draft version of our manuscript; Christine Ling for her careful work and creativity in typing various sections of the manuscript; Roslyn Tsao for her innovative suggestions, especially her idea for the title of this book; the staff of Carswell, particularly, Bernie Aron, Elio Ennamorati, Elizabeth Gillen, and Michael Silverstein for their enthusiasm and hard work; and, most of all, our parents for their loving support.

Summary of Chapters

For detailed Table of Contents, see opposite page.

Dedication iii
Foreword... v
Acknowledgments.. vii
Chapter 1. **Introduction** 1
    2. **Essential Background** 3
    3. **The Legal Research Checklist** 21
    4. **Canadian Encyclopedic Digest**.................... 33
    5. **Treatises**....................................... 37
    6. **Legal Periodicals** 39
    7. **Conference and Seminar Materials** 43
    8. **Law Reform Commission Reports** 45
    9. **Looseleaf Services**.............................. 47
    10. **Law Reports** 51
    11. **Canadian Abridgment**........................... 55
    12. **Research Tools for Accessing Unreported Decisions**................................... 67
    13. **Legal Dictionaries (Words and Phrases)**........... 71
    14. **Constitutional Research** 73
    15. **Researching Statutes** 87
    16. **Researching Regulations**........................ 97
    17. **Other Legal Research Tools**..................... 103
    18. **English Legal Research**........................ 109
    19. **American Legal Research**....................... 115
    20. **Guidelines for Writing Legal Essays, Case Comments and Legal Memoranda**.............. 127

Selective Topical Bibliography 141
Index 195

Table of Contents

Dedication.. iii
Foreword.. v
Acknowledgments.. vii

Chapter 1   **Introduction** 1

Chapter 2   **Essential Background**............................. 3
        Introduction....................................... 3
        Primary and Secondary Sources of Law Defined 3
        The Relative Weight of Primary Sources of Law 4
            Legislation 4
                The Constitution 4
                Statutes..................................... 5
                Regulations 5
            Jurisprudence 5
                Judicial Decisions........................... 5
                Decisions of Administrative Tribunals 6
                Role of Concurring and Dissenting
                Opinions..................................... 6
        Importance of Jurisdiction.......................... 6
        Importance of Court Structure....................... 7
            Federal Court System 7
            Provincial Court System......................... 7
            How a Case Makes its Way Through the Court
            Structure 8
        Prioritizing the Law 9
        Flow Chart for Prioritizing the Law 11
        Appendix I: Canadian Court System Chart 12

Chapter 3   **The Legal Research Checklist**.................... 21
        The Function of the Checklist...................... 21
            Research Guide and Record of Your Research
            Path 21
            Using the Research Checklist With the Flow Chart
            for Prioritizing the Law...................... 22
        How is the Checklist Organized? 22
        Description of Issue(s)............................ 23
        Research Tools 23
            Canadian Encyclopedic Digest 23

Treatises 23
Periodicals 24
Conference and Seminar Materials 24
Law Reform Commission Reports 24
Looseleaf Services. 24
Topical Law Reports. 25
Canadian Abridgment 25
Unreported Decisions 25
Noting Up Cases 26
Legal Dictionaries 26
The Constitution 26
Statutes 26
Regulations. 26
Other Legal Research Tools. 27
English and American Legal Research 27
Appendix I: Research Checklist 28

Chapter 4   **Canadian Encyclopedic Digest** 33
What is the Canadian Encyclopedic Digest? 33
When is the C.E.D. Useful? 33
How is the C.E.D. Organized? 33
How to Use the C.E.D. 34
Using the C.E.D. in Conjunction With the
Abridgment 35

Chapter 5   **Treatises** 37
What is a Treatise? 37
When is a Treatise Useful? 37
How to Use a Treatise 37
Using Treatises in Conjunction With the Abridgment . . . 38

Chapter 6   **Legal Periodicals** 39
What are Periodicals? 39
When are Periodicals Useful? 39
How are Periodicals Indexed? 39
How to Find Periodical Articles 41
How to Find Case Comments 41
When You Know the Case Name 41
When You Know the Subject but not the Case
Name 41
Commentary on Supreme Court of Canada
Decisions 41

Chapter 7   **Conference and Seminar Materials** 43
What are Conference and Seminar Materials? 43
When are Conference and Seminar Materials Useful? ... 43
How to Find Conference and Seminar Materials........ 43

Chapter 8   **Law Reform Commission Reports** 45
What are Law Reform Commission Reports? 45
When are Law Reform Commission Reports Useful? ... 45
How to Find Law Reform Commission Reports 46

Chapter 9   **Looseleaf Services** 47
What is a Looseleaf Service? 47
When are Looseleaf Services Useful? 48
How to Use a Looseleaf Service 48
Commerce Clearing House ("C.C.H.") Looseleafs:
   An Illustration 49
   How to Determine if a C.C.H. Looseleaf Exists in
      the Area You are Researching 49
   How are C.C.H. Looseleafs Indexed? 49
   Subject. 50
   Case Name 50
   Number 50
   Use of Paragraph Numbers. 50
   How are C.C.H. Looseleafs Updated? 50

Chapter 10   **Law Reports** 51
What are Law Reports? 51
How are Law Reports Organized? 52
When are Report Series Useful for Research
   Purposes? 53
How to Use a Law Report 53
   Finding Cases on a Subject 53
   Locating a Case When You Do Not Know the
      Citation But You Do Know that the Case is
      Reported in a Particular Series. 54

Chapter 11   **Canadian Abridgment** 55
What is the Canadian Abridgment? 55
How is the Abridgment Organized? 55
   Case Digests. 55
   Canadian Case Citations. 56
   Judicial Consideration of Statutes and Rules of
      Practice 57

Judicial Interpretation of Words & Phrases 57
All Available Citations for a Case 57
Legal Literature 58
How to Use the Various Sections of the Abridgment 58
Case Digests 58
Canadian Case Citations (How to Note Up Cases) ... 59
Judicial Treatment of Statutes on Rules of Practice
    (Noting Up a Statute or Rule) 61
Words and Phrases 63
Finding Case Citations 63
Index to Canadian Legal Literature 63
Canadian Law Online 63
Appendix 1: Canadian Abridgment Quick Reference
    Chart 65

Chapter 12   **Research Tools for Accessing Unreported**
Decisions 67
What are Unreported Decisions? 67
When are Unreported Decisions Useful? 67
Research Tools 67
How to Use the Research Tools 69
Legal Database Systems 69
A.C.W.S. and *W.C.B.* 69
A.W.L.D. and *B.C.W.L.D.* 69
B.C.D.C.C.C., B.C.D.C.S.C., O.D.C.C.C., and
    O.D.C.S.C. 69
Lawyer's Weekly 70
S.C.C.R.S. 70

Chapter 13   **Legal Dictionaries (Words and Phrases)** 71
What are Legal Dictionaries? 71
When do You Use Legal Dictionaries? 71
Research Tools 71
Canadian Abridgment (the "*Abridgment*") 71
Sanagan, *The Encyclopedia of Words and Phrases,*
    Legal Maxims, Canada 1825 to 1985, 4th ed...... 72
Carswell Topical Report Services 72
Yogis, *A Canadian Law Dictionary 1983* 72
Black's Law Dictionary, 1983 72

Chapter 14   **Constitutional Research** 73
What is Constitutional Research? 73
Researching Under the *Constitution Act, 1867* 74

Interpretation of a Constitutional Provision. 74
Historical Element. 74
Government Policy and Social Science
Evidence 76
Researching Under the *Charter of Rights and*
Freedoms 76
Structure of the *Charter* 76
Part I: Application 77
Part II: Substantive Rights and Freedoms 77
Part III: Governments' Rights to Limit
Substantive Rights and Freedoms. 77
Part IV: Remedies Available. 77
Stages of Research. 78
Does the *Charter* apply? 78
Does the Party have Standing to Bring a *Charter*
Claim? 79
Is there a *Charter* Infringement? 79
Is the Infringement Justified Under s. 1? 81
Tracing the History of the Impugned
Legislation. 82
Hansard 82
Law Reform Commission Reports and Royal
Commission Reports 83
Social Science Research 83
Legislation from Other Jurisdictions 84
What is the Appropriate Remedy? 85

Chapter 15 **Researching Statutes** 87
What are Statutes? 87
How are Statutes Made and Amended? 87
When is a Statute "in force"? 88
How are Statutes Published? 88
Sessional or Annual Volumes 88
Revised Statutes. 89
Statute Citators. 89
Doing Statutory Research 89
Step One: How to Determine whether a Statute
Exists. 90
Texts and Encyclopedias 90
Table of Public Statutes. 90
Step Two: How to Locate Statutes 90
Looseleafs and Office Consolidations 90
Step Three: Updating your Statutes 91

Federal Statutes.............................. 91
British Columbia Statutes 91
Nova Scotia Statutes......................... 92
Ontario Statutes............................. 93
Step Four: Statutory Interpretation 93
Judicial Consideration 93
Tracing the History of a Statute or Statutory
  Section 94
Interpretation Acts 94
Rules of Statutory Interpretation 95
Words and Phrases 95
Hansard 95

Chapter 16 **Researching Regulations** 97
What are Regulations? 97
How are Regulations Published?................... 97
When is a Regulation in Force? 97
Doing Regulatory Research........................ 98
Step One: How to Determine whether a Regulation
  Exists and Locate it........................ 98
Looseleaf Version of Statutes and Regulations.... 98
Using the Statutes, Orders and Regulations
  Portion of the Gazette...................... 98
Step Two: How to Update Regulations............. 98
Federal Regulations 99
British Columbia Regulations.................. 99
Nova Scotia Regulations 99
Ontario Regulations 100
Step Three: Interpreting Regulations 101

Chapter 17 **Other Legal Research Tools** 103
Government Telephone Directories 103
Databases of Memoranda of Law 104
Legal Publishers' Mailing Lists 104
Social Science Research........................... 104
Specialized Industrial Periodicals.................. 105
Press Reports..................................... 105
Reports on On-Going Litigation 106
Reports on How Other Cases have Settled......... 106
Reports on Similar Fact Situations 106
Background on Clients or Potential Clients, Other
  Parties, Lawyers, and Judges 106
Martindale-Hubbell Law Directory................. 106

Profiles 106
International Law Digest Volume 106
Listing of all Judges in U.S. Federal Court System
    and Text of the Uniform Acts and A.B.A. Codes.. 107

Chapter 18 **English Legal Research** 109
Introduction.................................. 109
Approaching English Legal Research. 109
The English Court Structure 109
Legal Encyclopedia 110
    Halsbury's Laws of England (3rd Edition) 110
    Halsbury's Laws of England (4th Edition)......... 110
Legal Periodicals.............................. 111
Legal Dictionaries and Words and Phrases
Encyclopedias 111
    Jowitt's Dictionary of English Law 111
    Stroud's Judicial Dictionary of Words and Phrases
        (4th ed.)................................ 111
    Words and Phrases Legally Defined (2nd ed.) 111
    Halsbury's Laws of England 111
Law Reports.................................. 111
    Locating Pre-1865 Cases 111
    Law Reports (Cases after 1865) 112
    All England Law Reports 112
    Topical Reports 112
The Digest: Annotated British, Commonwealth, and
    European Cases (formerly the English and Empire
    Digest) 113
Noting Up English Case Law 113
Statutes and Statutory Instruments (Regulations)...... 113
    Older Statutes............................... 113
    Statutes Currently in Force.................... 114
    Regulations................................. 114
    Halsbury's Statutory Instruments.............. 114

Chapter 19 **American Legal Research** 115
Introduction.................................. 115
Approaching American Legal Research.............. 115
The American Court Structure 115
Legal Encyclopedias............................ 116
    Corpus Juris Secundum (West Publishing
        Company) 116

American Jurisprudence 2nd (Lawyer's
Cooperative Publishing Company) 117
American Jurisprudence Proof of Facts 2nd
(Lawyer's Cooperative Publishing Co.) 117
American Law Reports ("A.L.R.") 118
Restatements of the Law 118
Legal Periodicals................................. 118
Legal Dictionaries and Words and Phrases
Encyclopedia.................................. 119
Law Reports.................................... 119
Digests 119
American Digest Sytem 120
Descriptive Word Approach 120
Topic Approach............................ 120
Case Name Approach....................... 121
Other Digests 121
Noting Up American Case Law................... 122
Statutes....................................... 123
Federal Statutes 123
State Statutes 123
Uniform Laws 123
Appendix I: Selective List of American Topical
Law Reports................................. 125

Chapter 20 **Guidelines for Writing: Legal Essays,
Case Comments and Legal Memoranda**........... 127
General Comments 127
Writing Style 127
Organization................................ 127
Use of Gender Neutral Language 128
Legal Essays 128
Case Comments............................... 129
Legal Memoranda............................. 130
Organization of a Legal Memorandum........... 131
Issues 131
Short Answer............................. 131
The Facts 132
The Law 132
Analysis 133
Conclusions.............................. 134
List of Authorities 134
Alternative Format 134

Appendix I: A Sample Legal Memorandum 135

Selective Topical Bibliography 141
    Administrative Law 141
    Banking Law 142
    Bankruptcy, Insolvency and Debtor-Creditor Law 143
    Civil Procedure 144
    Competition Law................................ 147
    Computer Law.................................. 147
    Conflict of Laws (Private International Law) 149
    Constitutional Law 149
    Contract Law.................................. 151
    Corporate Law................................. 152
    Criminal Law.................................. 155
    Damages...................................... 160
    Environmental Law.............................. 161
    Estates, Trusts and Wills 163
    Evidence...................................... 165
    Family Law 166
    Health Law 170
    Immigration and Refugee Law 171
    Injunctions.................................... 172
    Insurance Law 172
    Intellectual Property Law......................... 174
    International Law 175
    Labour and Employment Law 177
    Landlord and Tenant Law 182
    Marine Law 182
    Municipal and Planning Law...................... 183
    Native Law 184
    Personal Property and Personal Property Security Law . 185
    Poverty Law................................... 186
    Racism and the Law 187
    Real Estate or Real Property Law 187
    Securities Law................................. 189
    Statutory Interpretation and Drafting 190
    Tax Law...................................... 190
    Tort Law 192
    Women and the Law............................ 193

Index 197

1

Introduction

The purpose of this book is to teach thorough and efficient legal research skills. It is our experience that many law students and articling students approach legal research by trial and error. Law schools focus on teaching substantive law and often spend inadequate time teaching effective legal research.

Legal research is a vital skill for law students and lawyers. Law clerks and some social science students can also benefit from effective legal research skills. Without sound legal research skills, the researcher will waste time in the library — time which could be better spent analyzing the research problem and thinking of a creative solution. In addition, when she completes the research, she will have a sinking feeling at the back of her mind that maybe she did not check all of the relevant sources and maybe she did not update the sources properly. Failure to consult all of the relevant sources and/or update them properly can have detrimental consequences. The law is always in a state of flux. Statutes can be amended, and courts are constantly issuing decisions which change the law. It is the daunting task of finding the law that this book addresses.

Preliminary to the consideration of research techniques and strategies is an understanding of the basic principles or mechanics of the legal system. The central question faced by the researcher is: "What is the law?". In Chapter Two, we discuss the sources of law and how they are prioritized and interpreted to answer this central question. The chapter concludes with a handy flow-chart that will help you to assess and weigh the various types of law. The flow-chart will also help you to determine when you have done enough research to answer your research problem. For instance, when is it necessary to look at law in other Canadian jurisdictions? When is it necessary to look at American or English law?

Legal research can be both difficult and intimidating if you do not know what resources are available, when they are useful, and how to use them. This book is organized around a checklist of what we believe to be the principal tools for thorough Canadian legal research. The big fear in legal research is that nagging question: "Is there something else out there?" Use of the checklist allows you to say: "No, I have been thorough." By learning how to use the various research tools on the checklist, as well as when their use is appropriate, you can become an efficient legal researcher who is both discriminating and thorough. The successful researcher has an instinct about where to look in the law library, and the technical skills to make effective use of the tools in the library.

Chapter Three gives a broad description of the checklist. Subsequent chapters of the book outline in simple, easy to follow terms, how and when to use the various resources on the checklist.

Recognizing that legal research is a process whose purpose is to answer a legal question, we have included a chapter on writing legal essays, case comments and legal research memoranda. Once you have completed the research process of collecting the relevant law in the library, you will often need to express the results of your research in written form. The chapter provides guidance to help ensure that your legal writing is organized in a logical, focused, and clear manner.

Our final chapter is a selective topical bibliography based on the types of resources highlighted in the checklist.

A discussion of civil law research is beyond the scope of this book. Mention is made of computer research, but this book does not outline how to use the various computer data bases. There are other sources which adequately teach computer research skills.[1]

Finally, this book does not deal with methods of legal citation — the correct nomenclature for statutes, regulations, and cases. There are several excellent books that deal exclusively with the subject of legal citation.[2]

---

1 Legal databases are run by private companies, each of which pubish users' manuals. Many database companies also provide lessons and will answer telephone inquiries.

2 For instance, see McGill Law Journal, *Canadian Guide to Uniform Legal Citation*, 3rd ed. (Toronto: Carswell, 1992).

2

Essential Background

INTRODUCTION

The purpose of this book is to teach legal research — how and when to use the various legal research tools. However, before beginning your actual research, there are certain basics you need to know about the nature of law and the legal system in order to be able to discriminate between law that is "binding" and law that is merely "persuasive". Law that is binding *must be followed* by the courts. Law that is persuasive may influence judicial decisions, but courts are *not required to follow* these decisions. It is not enough to simply know how to locate cases, statutes, and textbooks on your topic. The researcher must be able to ascertain what law is binding in his or her jurisdiction. In addition, when the case law and the wording of a statute on a given topic seem to be in conflict, the researcher must be able to determine which takes precedence.

This chapter aims to provide the researchers with the background they need to assess when law is binding and when law is merely persuasive. The following topics will be examined:

1. What is the difference between primary and secondary sources of law?
2. What weight is attributed to the various types of primary sources of law?
3. How does jurisdiction impact on whether or not law is binding?
4. How does court structure impact on whether or not law is binding?

A flow-chart summarizing the concepts in this chapter and their applications to your research is provided.

For anyone who has had legal training, the information contained in this chapter may seem second nature. However, for those who are just beginning law school, or for those who are trained in other disciplines and require some legal research skills, this chapter will provide information that is essential to legal research.

PRIMARY AND SECONDARY SOURCES OF LAW DEFINED

Primary sources of law consist of statutes, regulations, judicial decisions, and decisions of administrative tribunals. These sources of law are the products of various government bodies, legislatures, courts and administrative tribunals.[1] When asked to do research on a problem, you will ultimately want to find primary sources of law on your topic. Secondary sources of law are written by lawyers — legal scholars and practitioners. They consist of legal encyclopedias, treatises, and journal articles. These sources of law collect, explain, and interpret primary sources of law and are a means of accessing primary sources.

Some secondary sources of law, such as a treatise or a journal article written by a well-respected scholar, may be persuasive in court and often such sources are cited in appellate decisions to interpret the law. Other secondary sources, such as legal encyclopedias, tend not to be regarded as persuasive and would rarely be referred to in a court decision.[2] They are merely useful finding tools which provide an overview of the law on numerous topics. Secondary sources of law, irrespective of their level of persuasiveness, are never binding and are not the law *per se*. When using secondary sources it is important to be aware of the biases of the particular author, and researchers should always ensure that they have read the cases and statutes cited in secondary sources for themselves, rather than relying on the author's interpretations of the law.

Unlike secondary sources, primary sources of law may be binding, depending on a number of factors such as jurisdiction and court level. Before discussing jurisdiction and court level, it is important to understand the relative weight of the various primary sources of law identified above — that is, when there are two different sources of primary law on the same topic, which takes precedence?

THE RELATIVE WEIGHT OF PRIMARY SOURCES OF LAW

Legislation

The Constitution

The Constitution[3] is the most important statute. All other law, whether enacted by parliament or made by judges, must be consistent with the Constitution. The Constitution governs the division of powers between the federal and provincial governments and bestows fundamental rights and freedoms on individuals and groups.

---

1 Strictly speaking administrative tribunal decisions are not law. See the section, later in this chapter, on "Decisions of Administrative Tribunals", where the status of such decisions is discussed.

2 *Halsbury's Laws of England* is the exception to this rule against the citation of legal encyclopedias. It is frequently cited.

3 *Constitution Act, 1867* (U.K.), 30 & 31 Vict., c. 3 and *Constitution Act*, 1982, being Schedule B to the *Canada Act 1982* (U.K.), 1982, c. 11.

Statutes

Statutes are laws that are passed by the legislature — federal or provincial. They usually deal with a specific subject. For example, the *Criminal Code*[4] is a comprehensive statute that defines criminal offences, prescribes punishments, and sets out the procedure for administering the *Code*. Assuming that a statute is consistent with the Constitution, it is the law in a given jurisdiction.[5] Statutes are, however, subject to interpretation by the judiciary and administrative tribunals.[6] Such interpretations form part of the law. Accordingly, statutory law can be altered by any of the following: (*a*) other acts of the legislature (amendments or repeals); (*b*) judicial or administrative tribunal interpretations; and (*c*) declarations of constitutional invalidity ("striking down").

Regulations

Statutes often empower administrative agencies to make rules ("regulations") which provide detail about how the statute is to be implemented. For example, a statute might say, "It is unlawful to pollute." Regulations might specify what substances constitute pollutants and the registration, licensing, and monitoring requirements for those who handle such pollutants. Regulations, therefore, provide detail that is not found in the statute in the form of: definitions, licensing requirements, registration requirements, insurance requirements, performance specifications, exemptions, forms, etc.

Jurisprudence

Judicial Decisions

Judicial decisions or "case law" are judge-made law. In the absence of a statute on the topic area, case law on the topic will be binding. Note that it cannot be any case law. In order to assess whether a particular decision is binding, you must pay attention to both jurisdiction and level of court. These topics are discussed below. The law in an area that is governed solely by case law is known as "common law".

Even where statutes exist, judge-made law is necessary to interpret what the words and phrases of the statute mean in relation to specific fact

---

4 R.S.C. 1985, c. C-46.

5 A statutory provision is binding and assumed to be constitutional unless a court has found it to be unconstitutional or "struck down" the provision.

6 Strictly speaking administrative tribunal decisions are not law. See the section, later in this chapter, on "Decisions of Administrative Tribunals", where the status of such decisions is discussed.

situations. Cases interpret a statute and form part of the law. In fact, if a court has ruled that a section of a statute is to be interpreted in a certain way, even if there are several other rational readings of the section, only the reading endorsed by the court is law.

Decisions of Administrative Tribunals

Administrative tribunals are not courts of law. Traditionally, they have been described as "creatures of statute". This means that their powers to adjudicate are based strictly on the wording of the enabling statute that created the tribunal.

Decisions of administrative tribunals are only meant to be binding on the parties to the particular case. Unlike judicial decisions, they are not "law" — that is, they are not binding precedents. However, in practice, previous decisions of the same tribunal will be very persuasive.

Role of Concurring and Dissenting Opinions

There are situations where the majority of the court agree to decide a case in a certain way and several judges write concurring opinions for the majority. These opinions may differ substantially in their reasoning. Such cases are troublesome to interpret because the exact law is not clearly defined. When dealing with these cases, your analysis must be sensitive to the reasoning employed in all of the concurring judgments.

Dissenting opinions are not binding. However, they can be persuasive depending on the judge.

IMPORTANCE OF JURISDICTION

Only statutes and case law within your jurisdiction are binding. A British Columbia statute, for instance, would never be binding in Nova Scotia. Similarly, a decision from the Saskatchewan Court of Appeal would never be binding in Alberta or any other province outside of Saskatchewan. However, if the same Saskatchewan Court of Appeal decision was appealed to the Supreme Court of Canada, the decision of the Supreme Court of Canada, although dealing with a case that arose in Saskatchewan, would be binding on all of Canada.

Decisions from other jurisdictions, while not binding, may be persuasive, depending on the level of court of the decision, the reputation of the judge or panel of judges who wrote the decision, and the actual jurisdiction. In Canada, the British Columbia and Ontario appellate courts are regarded as very persuasive throughout the country. This is not to say that decisions of these courts will necessarily be followed elsewhere. Yet it is not unusual for courts of other provinces to at least consider decisions from these courts.

Foreign law, while never binding in Canada, may also be persuasive. When an area of Canadian law has not been well developed or is in a state of confusion, courts will often look to the case law of other jurisdictions, particularly Britain and the United States, about a rational approach to the legal problem.

Statutes from other jurisdictions are generally not persuasive. However, there are some exceptions. If another jurisdiction has a similar statute, judicial interpretation of that statute may be relevant persuasive authority. For example, many provinces have similar business corporations legislation. Accordingly, cases decided under one province's statute may be persuasive authority when considering the interpretation of another province's statute. An American example is the Uniform Commercial Code, a comprehensive code dealing with commercial law, that has been passed by many state legislatures. Treatises and articles will identify these similar statutory regimes for you.

IMPORTANCE OF COURT STRUCTURE

The court structure is hierarchical. The basic rule is that given two decisions from two different levels of court, the decision from the higher court is binding. It is, therefore, essential to know the court structure of the jurisdiction for which you are doing research.

In Canada there are two main court systems — federal and provincial. The highest court in both of these systems is the Supreme Court of Canada. Below is a general overview of the Canadian court structure.[7]

Federal Court System

The federal court system consists of the Federal Court (trial division) and an appellate court called the Federal Court of Appeal. Appeals from the Federal Court of Appeal are heard in the Supreme Court of Canada.

Provincial Court System

The provincial court system comprises a provincial "superior" court of general jurisdiction[8] and an appellate court usually called the Court of

---

7 For a more specific description of the court structure in your province or territory, consult the chart from the *Canadian Abridgment* reproduced in Appendix I.

8 The names of the provincial superior courts vary from province to province: in Alberta, British Columbia, Manitoba, New Brunswick, and Saskatchewan, they are called the Court of Queen's Bench; in Newfoundland, Northwest Territories, Nova Scotia, Prince Edward Island, and Yukon Territory, they are called the Supreme Court; in Ontario it is called the Ontario Court (General Division); and in Quebec, it is called the Superior Court.

Appeal.[9] Appeals from the provincial courts of appeal are heard in the Supreme Court of Canada.

Each province also has "inferior" provincial courts. The judges of these courts are provincially appointed, in contrast to the judges of the above mentioned courts who are all federally appointed. The provincial inferior courts have civil, criminal and, in some provinces, family and youth court divisions. The civil courts are small claims courts, which hear civil cases where the amount claimed or value of property in question does not exceed specified amounts. The criminal courts deal with less serious criminal offences. The pathway of appeals from the inferior provincial courts are determined by the specific statutory provisions regulating the litigation.

How a Case Makes its Way Through the Court Structure

The majority of cases are the result of opposing parties resolving a conflict over:

(*a*) the constitutionality of a statute;
(*b*) the legality of an action or activity;
(*c*) an entitlement to compensation or to a remedial order for an action or activity;
(*d*) an entitlement to property; or
(*e*) the rights and obligations between parties.

When the parties litigate, a trial is held and a decision rendered by a judge or a judge and jury. The court in which the trial is held is referred to as the court of first instance. Often this decision will be the final one. However, should one of the parties be dissatisfied with the decision and if that party has a right of appeal, he or she may choose to appeal some or all of the legal and/or factual issues in his or her case to the next level of court. The decision of the appeal court will take precedence over the decision of the trial court.

It may be possible to appeal the decision of an appeal court further. Any subsequent appeal(s) will displace those decisions preceding them in the appeal process, unless the decision is affirmed (i.e., the appeal court decides that the decision of the lower court was correct).

It should be kept in mind that the right to appeal does not exist for every case. For any given case, any one of four situations is possible:

(*a*) a right of appeal;

---

9 In Alberta, British Columbia, Manitoba, New Brunswick, Northwest Territories, Ontario, Saskatchewan, and Yukon Territory, the appellate court is called the Court of Appeal. In Newfoundland, Nova Scotia, and Prince Edward Island, the appellate court is called the Court of Appeal.

(*b*) a right to seek leave to appeal (where the appeal court, after hearing submissions, decides whether it will hear the appeal);

(*c*) no right of appeal; or

(*d*) no further appeal because there is no higher court.

PRIORITIZING THE LAW

The principles for determining precedence among sources of law discussed in this chapter translate into a hierarchy. Set out below is a flow chart that will help you to identify what, if any, binding law there is on a given topic area and to assess the relative persuasiveness of various sources of law. A common complaint of law students is, "I don't know when to stop my research." Often students do more research than is required to analyze the problem they have been assigned. The flow chart helps you to know when you have done enough research to answer your research question effectively.

Beware, however, that sometimes the objective of your research is broader than answering a legal question. For instance, if you are writing a law school essay or journal article, you may be interested in examining the need for legal reform in a particular area of law. If this is the case, you will probably want to look at all of the sources of law identified on the flow chart. The flow chart is organized to give you a sense of what the law is. Essays and articles often focus not on what the law is but on what it should be. In considering what the law should be, your research will often encompass all sources identified on the flow chart.

Statutes are the first reference on the flow chart. When researching a legal problem, your first objective is to determine whether a statute or statutes exist on the topic. If there is a statute which contains the answer, your research will be complete once you have checked for judicial consideration of the relevant statutory provision. If there is not a statute on your topic, look for judicial decisions in your jurisdiction, preferably from the Supreme Court of Canada or the Court of Appeal, as these will be binding. If you cannot find decisions from an appellate court in your jurisdiction, look for lower court decisions. Decisions of lower courts may or may not be binding. Sometimes you will find two or more decisions of a lower court (*e.g.* the Ontario Court (General Division)) which reach different conclusions on the same legal question. All of these decisions cannot be binding, and it is unclear which decision will be authoritative in a given case. Other times, decisions of lower courts are widely followed and viewed as binding.

The upper portion of the flow chart, which depicts binding sources of law, is an accurate schema of the rigid hierarchy that exists at the heart of the common law system. Although the bottom portion of the flow chart also suggests a hierarchy, the hierarchy is in fact much more fluid. For example we have classified appellate court decisions from other Canadian jurisdictions as the first item in the persuasive portion of the flow chart. However, in some instances, a treatise or article by a well-respected scholar or an English or American decision may be more persuasive.

The essence of the common law system is change through confrontation. The common law evolves because parties fight over what the law is. Use of the flow chart is meant to clarify the task of interpreting the law, but it is not intended to induce a passive attitude. You should always keep in mind that the law can be changed through the creative use of persuasive authority. Accordingly, if the law appears to be unfavourable to your client, and it is not absolutely binding, you should strive to find any credible persuasive authority that bolsters an interpretation more conducive to the needs of your client. Moreover, even if there is binding authority, you may be able to distinguish your case on the facts.

FLOW CHART FOR PRIORITIZING THE LAW

Is there a Statute?   ⟶ if yes ⟶   Check for Judicial
Consideration
(See Chapter Eleven)

↓

If No
↓

Is there Case Law from the   ⟶ if yes ⟶   Note-up this case law
Supreme Court of Canada on   (See Chapter Eleven)
your topic?

↓

If No
↓

Is there Case Law from the   ⟶ if yes ⟶   Note-up this case law
Court of Appeal in your   (See Chapter Eleven)
jurisdiction?

↓

If No
↓

                                      BINDING

....

↓

Is there Case Law from lower   MAY BE BINDING
courts in your jurisdiction?

If No   PERSUASIVE
_____

↓

Is there Case Law from   ⟶ if yes ⟶   Note-up this case law
appellate courts in other   (See Chapter Eleven)
Canadian Jurisdictions?

↓

If No
↓

Are there Canadian Treatises or Periodicals
on your topic by well-regarded legal scholars?

↓

If No
↓

Is there Case Law from   ⟶ if yes ⟶   Note-up this case law
lower courts in other   (See Chapter Eleven)
Canadian Jurisdictions?

↓

If No
↓

Is there Case Law from   ⟶ if yes ⟶   Note-up this case law
appellate courts in England   (See Chapters Eighteen and
and/or the United States?   Nineteen)

↓

If No
↓

Are there English and/or American Treatises
or Periodicals on your topic?

Appendix I

CANADIAN COURT SYSTEM

The following is an overview in two parts of the Canadian court system from the beginning of British settlement to date. The first part shows the Courts of the Provinces, with courts currently in existence in bold face; the second shows the federal courts, with a brief description of their jurisdictions. It is provided for reference when assessing the weight to be given to any given case, and for aid when the case law deals with procedural issues which may depend upon the court structures in existence at the time. All footnotes can be found at the end of this section.

Jurisdiction	Justices, Magistrates and Provincial Courts[1]	County and District Courts	Surrogate and Probate Courts
Alberta	**Justices of the Peace (1835-)** Magistrates' Court (1918-1978) **Provincial Court (Civil Division) (1978-) Provincial Court (Criminal Division)(1978-) Provincial Court(Small Claims Division) (1978-)**	District Court (1907-1978)	**Surrogate Court (1967-)**
British Columbia	**Justices of the Peace (1835-)** Small Debt Court (1895-1969) **Provincial Court (1969-)**	Vancouver Island District Court (1853-1867) British Columbia County Court (1859-1990)	
Manitoba	**Justices of the Peace (1835-)** Magistrates' Court (1916-1972) **Provincial Court (1972-)**	County Court (1872-1984)	Surrogate Court (1881-1984)
New Brunswick	**Justices of the Peace (1786-)** Parish Court (1876-1942) Magistrates' Court (1942-1969) **Provincial Court (1969-)**	Inferior Court of Common Pleas (1785-1867) County Court (1867-1979)	**Probate Court (1786-)**

Provincial Superior Courts Trial Divisions[2]	Courts of Appeal[3]	Family and Youth Courts	Admiralty Courts[4]
Supreme Court Trial Division (1907-1978) **Court of Queen's Bench (1978-)**	**Supreme Court Appeal Division (1919-)**	**Provincial Court (Family Division) (1978-) Provincial Court (Youth Division) (1978-)**	
Supreme Court of Vancouver Island (1853-1870) **Supreme Court of British Columbia (1859-)**	Supreme Court *en banc* (1872-1906) **Court of Appeal (1909-)**		Vancouver Island Vice-Admiralty Court (1849-1891) British Columbia Vice-Admiralty Court (?-1866)
General Court of Assiniboia (1835-1872) **Court of Queen's Bench (1872-)**	Supreme Court *en banc* (1872-1906) **Court of Appeal (1906-)**	**Provincial Court (Family Division) (1984-)**	
Supreme Court (1785-1909) Law only until 1854 Court of Chancery (1838-1854) Equity Supreme Court (Queen's Bench Division) (1909-1966) Law only Supreme Court (Chancery Side) (1909-1966) Equity **Court of Queen's Bench (1966-)**	Supreme Court *en banc* (1785-1909) Supreme Court (Chancery Division) (1909-1966) **Court of Appeal (1966-)**	Court of Divorce and Matrimonial Causes (1860-1948) **Court of Queen's Bench (Family Division) (1978-)**	Vice-Admiralty Court (1787-1891)

Jurisdiction	Justices, Magistrates and Provincial Courts[1]	County and District Courts	Surrogate and Probate Courts
Newfoundland	Justices of the Peace (1728-) Stipendiary Magistrates (1858-1974) District Courts (1869-1949) **Provincial Court (1974-)**	District Court (1949-1986)	
Nova Scotia	**Justices of the Peace (1727-)** Civil Court (1727-1749) Municipal Court (1895-1958) **Provincial Court (1958-)**	County Court of the City of Halifax (1749-1752) Inferior Court of Common Pleas (1752-1841) Court of Sessions (1841-1876) **County Court (1876-)**	Probate Court (1759-1897)
Ontario*	**Justices of the Peace (1764-)** Magistrates' Court (1849-1968) Provincial Court (Criminal Division) (1968-1990) Court of Requests (1792-1841) Division Court (1841-1970) Small Claims Court (1970-1984) Provincial Court (Civil Division)(1984-1990) General [Quarter] Sessions of the Peace (1777-1984) **Ontario Court of Justice (Provincial Division) (1990-) Ontario Court of Justice (General Division); Small Claims Court (1990-)**	District Court (1794-1849), (1984-1990) County Court (1849-1984)	Surrogate Court (1793-1990) Probate Court (1793-1858)

Provincial Superior Courts Trial Divisions[2]	Courts of Appeal[3]	Family and Youth Courts	Admiralty Courts[4]
Supreme Court (1793-) Surrogates' Courts (1793-1834)	Supreme Court *en banc* (1793-1986) **Court of Appeal (1986-)**	**Unified Family Court (1978-)**	Vice-Admiralty Court (1743-1891)
Governor in Council (1721-1749) General Court (1749-1754) Supreme Court (1754-) Law only until 1857, and from 1864-1884 Court of Chancery (1825-1857) (1864-1884) Equity Supreme Court of Cape Breton (?-1820) Law only	Supreme Court en banc (1754-1966) **Supreme Court Appellate Division (1966-)**	Divorce Court (1866-1948) **Family Court (1963-)**	Vice-Admiralty Court (1739-1891)
Court of Common Pleas (1788-1794) Law only Supreme Court (Queen's Bench Division)(1794-1913) Law only Supreme Court (Chancery Division) (1837-1913) Equity Supreme Court (Common Pleas Division)(1849-1913) Law only Supreme Court (Exchequer Division) (1903-1913) Law only Supreme Court (High Court of Justice) (1913-1990) **Supreme Court in Bankruptcy (1913-) Jurisdiction conferred by Bankruptcy Act (Federal) Ontario Court of Justice (General Division) (1990-)**	Court of Error and Appeal (1849-1881) Court of Appeal (1881-1913) Divisional Courts of Appellate Division (1913-1931) **Court of Appeal (1931-) Divisional Court** (1881-1913) **(1972-)**	Provincial Court (Family Division) (1968-1990) **Unified Family Court of Hamilton-Wentworth (1976-) Ontario Court of Justice (Provincial Division) (1990-)**	Maritime Court (1877-1891)

Jurisdiction	Justices, Magistrates and Provincial Courts[1]	County and District Courts	Surrogate and Probate Courts
P.E.I.	Justices of the Peace (1773-) Small Debt Commissioners (1832-1873) Stipendiary Magistrates (?-1974) **Provincial Court (1974-)**	County Court (1873-1975)	Probate Court (1772-1937)
Québec	**Juge de paix (1764-)** Cour des Sessions de la Paix (1777-1988) Cours des Requêtes (1770-1793) Juge provincial (1794-1843) Cour du Banc du Roi en "terme inférieur" (1794-1849) Cour de Circuit (1794-1953) Cour des Commissaires (1807-1839), (1843-1963) Cour des Magistrats (1869-1965) Cour provinciale (1965-1988) **Cour du Québec (1988-)**		
Saskatchewan	**Justices of the Peace (1873-)** Magistrates' Court (1913-1978) **Provincial Court (1978-)**	District Court (1907-1981)	**Surrogate Court (1907-)**
Northwest Territories	**Justices of the Peace (1873-)** Stipendiary Magistrates (1873-1887), (1907-1956) **Territorial Court (1978-)**		
Yukon Territory	**Justices of the Peace (1873-)** **Territorial Court (1983-)**		

Provincial Superior Courts Trial Divisions[2]	Courts of Appeal[3]	Family and Youth Courts	Admiralty Courts[4]
Supreme Court Trial Division (1770-) Law only until 1975 Court of Chancery (1848-1975) Equity	Supreme Court *en banc* (1770-1987) Court of Appeal (Equity) (1869-1975) Equity **Supreme Court Appeal Division (1987-)**	Supreme Court (Family Division) (1975-)	
Cour du Banc du Roi (1764-1777) Common Law Cour du Banc du Roi (1777-1794) Criminal Law only Cour des plaids communs (1764-1794) Cour du Banc du Roi (1794-1849) **Cour Supérieure (1849-)**	Cour d'Appel (1843-1849) Cour du Banc de la Reine (1849-1965) **Cour d'Appel (1967-)** Cour de Révision (1864-1920)	Tribunal de la jeunesse (1980-1988) **Cour du Québec (1988-)**	Cour de Vice-Admirauté (1764-1891)
Supreme Court (1907-1918) **Court of Queen's Bench (1918-)**	Supreme Court *en banc* (1907-1915) **Court of Appeal (1915-)**	**Unified Family Court (1978-)**	
Supreme Court (1978-) (1887-1907) Territorial Court (1956-1978)	Prior to 1960, appeals to Alberta Supreme Court Appeal Division **Court of Appeal (1960-)**		
Territorial Court (1898-1985) **Supreme Court (1983-)**	Prior to 1960, appeals to British Columbia Court of Appeal **Court of Appeal (1960-)**		

Federal Courts

Although matters arising under federal law are in general dealt with by the Superior Courts of the Provinces, there are a number of exceptions to this general rule which are dealt with by a separate structure of federal Courts.

Subject Matter	Original Jurisdiction	Appeal Jurisdiction
Intellectual Property Admiralty ⁶Litigation involving the Crown in right of Canada, concurrent with provincial Superior Courts Appeals from Federal Tribunals under the *Income Tax Act* and *Estate Tax Act*	**Exchequer Court of Canada** (1875-1970) **Federal Court Trial Division** **(1970-)** **⁵Tax Court of Canada** **(1983-)**	**Federal Court of Appeal** **(1970-)**
Appeals from Federal Tribunals under the *Citizenship Act* ⁶Review of Federal Tribunals under s. 18 of the *Federal Court Act* relief in the nature of injunction, prerogative remedies or declaration References from Federal Tribunals under s. 18.1 of the *Federal Court Act*.	**Federal Court Trial Division** **(1970-)**	**Federal Court of Appeal** **(1970-)**
Appeals from Federal Tribunals under other specific statutes ⁶Review of Federal Tribunals listed in s. 28 of the *Federal Court Act*: judicial review of quasi-judicial tribunals	**Federal Court of Appeal** **(1970-)**	
Appeals from Courts Martial	**Court Martial Appeal Board** (1950-1959) **Court Martial Appeal Court** **(1959-)**	

*The Courts of Justice Amendment Act, 1989 made the following changes in the Ontario court system:
1) the Court of Appeal is confirmed as the final court of appeal for the province and is separated from the High Court;
2) a new superior court is established, known as the Ontario Court of Justice, composed of two divisions - the General Division and the Provincial Division;
3) the Ontario Court (General Division) combines the jurisdiction formerly exercised by the High Court, the District Court and the surrogate courts. The Divisional Court is continued as a branch of the Ontario Court (General Division). The Small Claims Court is also a branch of the Ontario Court (General Division);
4) the Ontario Court (Provincial Division) combines the jurisdiction formerly exercised by the Provincial Court (Criminal Division), the Provincial Court (Family Division) and the Provincial Offences Court;
5) the Unified Family Court is established as a superior court but is otherwise not changed.

[1]In addition to the courts listed above, some of the older provinces have municipal and local courts of a magistrates' level in the more major cities.

[2]Except where otherwise noted, all Courts have jurisdiction over both law and equity.

[3]The Supreme Court of Canada is the final court of appeal from judgments of all provincial and federal courts. All of the older colonies had appeals to the governor in Council (in the Maritimes, callled the Court of Error and Appeal, not to be confused with the Ontario court of the same name). These died out when the Privy Council began to accept appeals from lower courts.

[4]When Great Britain handed its admiralty jurisdiction over to Canada in 1891, the Exchequer Court assumed the admiralty jurisdicton which remains with the Federal Court.

[5]Pursuant to the *Tax Court Amendment Act*, R.S.C. 1985 (4th Supp.), c. 51 the Tax Court of Canada has exclusive original jurisdiction to hear and determine references and appeals on matters involving the *Income Tax Act* and certain other Acts. Appeals from decisions of the Tax Court of Canada go directly to the Federal Court of Appeal and not to the Federal Court, Trial Division.

[6]Jurisdictions given reflect the amendments to the *Federal Court Act* - the *Federal Court Amendment Act*, S.C. 1990, c. 8, to which Royal Assent was given on March 29, 1990 and which is to come into force on proclamation.

3

The Legal Research Checklist

You will note that there is a checklist in Appendix I to this chapter. We suggest that you turn to the checklist now and scan it quickly. This will give you a better sense of what this chapter is about.

FUNCTION OF THE CHECKLIST

Research Guide and Record of Your Research Path

Every research problem is different; however, the checklist outlines a logical way of approaching all research problems. By using it, your familiarity with the tools of legal research will be enhanced. We suggest photocopying it and using it to guide your research. It will serve a dual purpose, by guiding the course of your research and providing a record of where you have looked. For particularly thorny research problems, the use of an unusual source is often heralded as a creative solution. The checklist will direct your mind to such sources.

Use of the checklist will enable you to keep a written record of your research path. If you have looked at a source under a certain heading and have found nothing, you should make a note of it on the checklist. A key research skill is keeping notes of what you have examined. It is easy to forget that you have looked at something, meaning that you duplicate your work, or worse yet, you mistakenly think that you have looked at something when you have not. You do not need to write detailed notes, but they should not just list the sources you relied on. Instead, you should enumerate the sources you discarded for irrelevance with brief reasons. This way, if you are subsequently asked why your memorandum did not include a certain case, you will have a note of it. In addition, sometimes the relevance of certain aspects of a case will become more apparent once you have delved into the topic. Your notes will help you to retrieve cases you mistakenly discarded. There will also be occasions when you will be asked to research a problem for which there is nothing in the library. In order to have confidence in the results of your research, in the event that you find nothing, you need to be able to prove that you have done a thorough search of the relevant sources.

Using the Research Checklist With the Flow Chart for Prioritizing the Law

The essence of legal research is relevance. While conducting your research, guided by the checklist, you need an understanding of the relative weight and persuasiveness of the sources of law. While examining the sources of law that you find with the checklist, it may be advisable to refer to the flow chart at the end of Chapter Two. The flow chart will give you an indication of how your research is progressing — have you found the answer — as well as providing a method of evaluating the sources of law that you find.

HOW IS THE CHECKLIST ORGANIZED?

The checklist is the skeleton of this book, listing in an organized fashion, the various sources that you need to access the law. The checklist is a list of legal resources based on our assessment of their usefulness. Although the coverage of legal research tools in this book is extensive, we have not tried to be absolutely comprehensive. Instead, we have selected the most useful legal research tools.

The checklist begins with the main secondary sources to law, as these serve as a means of accessing and interpreting primary sources of law. General or broad secondary sources, such as legal encyclopedias, are discussed first. Specific secondary sources, such as treatises and periodicals, are discussed next. After specific secondary sources, the checklist enumerates primary sources of law — cases, statutes, and regulations — and how to update them.[1] The order of the items on the checklist reflect what is usually the most logical and efficient sequence of approaching your research.

Keep in mind that you will not need to look at every item on the checklist for every research problem. The instructions in this book, concerning the use of each item on the checklist, will teach you when their use is necessary. For example you may be referred to the leading case in the topic area. In that situation, you would begin your research by reading the case and the sources that the case cited. You would also note-up the case to see how it has been considered by subsequent courts. For other research problems, the most efficient approach may begin with a phone call to the relevant government ministry. This chapter gives a brief overview of each of the sections on the checklist. The remaining chapters of this book flesh out the various parts of the checklist.

---

1 See Chapter Two for a discussion of the distinction between primary and secondary sources of law.

DESCRIPTION OF ISSUE(S)

At the top of the checklist, we have left space for you to identify the issues or describe the topic that you are researching. This is important because the way you phrase the issue sets the parameters for your research. The ability to identify the legal issues raised in a factual situation is a complex skill that is acquired through legal training at law school. However, since legal research often involves delving into areas of the law with which the researcher has never had contact, the issue may not be obvious at the outset. Accordingly, the sources listed on the checklist may be helpful in formulating the issues, particularly the *Canadian Encyclopedic Digest* and any treatises on your topic.

You should also keep in mind that you may have identified the issue but not in the vocabulary used in the legal literature. For example your issue may deal with the person responsible for paying a courier. If you try to answer this question by looking under "couriers", you will find nothing. There is, however, a well developed body of law dealing with "carriers". In phrasing your issue, you should be sensitive to the terminology; and before you conclude that there is nothing on an issue, consider whether the answer is under a synonym for the term that you were searching. Did you formulate the issue using the correct legal terminology? In essence, do some brain storming at the outset of the research process.

RESEARCH TOOLS

Canadian Encyclopedic Digest

The *Canadian Encyclopedic Digest* is a legal encyclopedia that contains narrative descriptions of various subject areas of the law. The descriptions are accompanied by footnotes that cite cases as authority for the content of the narrative. There are two *Canadian Encyclopedic Digests*, one for Ontario law (*C.E.D. (Ont.* 3rd)) and one for the law of the Western provinces (*C.E.D. (West)* (3rd)). Federal law is covered in both *C.E.D.*'s. The *C.E.D.* is a useful place to begin your research, particularly if you know little about the topic or area of law you have been asked to research. It will provide you with a broad overview of the topic before you delve into the subtleties.

Treatises

Treatises are texts on areas of the law. They give a more detailed interpretation and discussion of the law than will be found in legal encyclopedias. Treatises should be consulted after you obtain an overview of your topic through a legal encyclopedia.

Periodicals

Periodicals contain articles on very specific areas of the law. They are a useful source for interpreting the law and often provide greater detail on specialized topics than treatises. Further, they frequently provide more current information than many treatises.

Conference and Seminar Materials

A number of organizations offer conferences and seminars for members of the legal profession and/or industry. These conferences generally include written material that summarizes and supplements the oral presentation. Conference and seminar materials generally focus on recent developments in the law and are geared towards practitioners.

Law Reform Commission Reports

Law reform commissions are independent legal think-tanks which study and publish reports on legal reform. The reports outline what the law is, demonstrate why the law should be reformed, and make concrete recommendations as to how the law can be reformed.

Law reform commission reports can be used to obtain an overview of selected legal and procedural topics. These reports are particularly useful when your research requires you to comment on legal reform.

Looseleaf Services

Looseleaf services are published in a binder format so that they can be updated regularly. Looseleaf services include:

(*a*) legal encyclopedias and other works which summarize the law in a particular area;
(*b*) consolidated versions of statutes or regulations;
(*c*) annotated statutes; and
(*d*) court forms and precedents.

The main advantage of looseleaf services is that they save time updating material. Looseleafs, as their name suggests, are published in binders so that new developments in the law can be inserted as they occur and obsolete law removed.

Once you have identified your issues and canvassed the law, you should always check to see if a looseleaf services exists on your topic.

Topical Law Reports

Topical law reports are report series that contain cases dealing with a specific area of the law. Topical law reports are a primary source of law, in that secondary sources will refer you to cases reported in them. However, topical law reports can also be viewed as an access tool because they are organized by topic. Accordingly, if you know that you need to find cases on a specific topic in an area of law for which there are topical law reports, the indexes of the reports will help you to access relevant law on your subject.

Canadian Abridgment

The *Canadian Abridgment* (the "*Abridgment*") is a comprehensive research tool. It allows you to research:

1. the law in a certain subject area (This feature is used when trying to collect the case law on a topic if treatises and the *Canadian Encyclopedic Digest* have not been helpful or if you want to be very thorough.);
2. the judicial consideration of a case (This feature of the *Abridgment* is used to determine how a case has been interpreted, applied or followed.);
3. the judicial consideration of a statute or rule of practice (This feature of the *Abridgment* is used to determine how a statute or rule of practice has been interpreted.);
4. the judicial consideration of a word or phrase (This is a tool for accessing words and phrases.);
5. secondary legal literature (periodical articles, treatises, and government publications) (The *Abridgment* offers one manner of accessing secondary legal literature.); and
6. all of the citations of a case (This is used to determine where a case has been reported).

Unreported Decisions

Unreported decisions, as their name suggests, are decisions that have not been published in a report series. There are two types of unreported decisions: (1) decisions that have just been released by a court and may or may not be reported in the future, and (2) older decisions that have never been reported. The first type of unreported decision will usually be more useful and will ensure that your research is up-to-date.

Noting Up Cases

Noting up a case involves finding the subsequent cases that have considered the case you are noting up. It is crucial to ensure that a case you are relying on has not been subsequently overturned. Even if the case has not been overturned, it is important to determine if and how your case has been considered, distinguished, applied, etc., by the courts. The *Canadian Case Citations: Cases Judicially Considered* portion of the *Abridgment* is used for this purpose. It may be supplemented with a computer data base search.

Legal Dictionaries

Legal Dictionaries let you research the meaning of certain legal terms and the legal interpretation of words and phrases. This can be useful when you are trying to interpret a statute for which there is no clear case law.

The Constitution

The Constitution is the supreme law of the country. All other laws are valid only to the extent that they are consistent with the Constitution. There are two main categories of constitutional research problems: federalism and rights and freedoms.

Statutes

Our law is composed of statutory law that is passed by the government and cases that are decided by the courts. Whenever there is a statute that handles an issue that you are researching, the statute, subject to any judicial interpretations, is always paramount. Statutes like the rest of the law are constantly changing. It is necessary to be able to find statutes relevant to your research, to ensure that the statute that you are using is up-to-date, and to find case law which has interpreted the various provisions of the statute. Judicial consideration of the statute can be found using the *Canadian Citations: Statutes Judicially Considered* portion of the *Abridgment* and one of the Statute Citator services.

Regulations

Regulations are passed under the authority of statutes and are similarly subject to judicial interpretation, but are much less frequently interpreted by the courts than statutes. Regulations are also constantly changing. It is necessary to be able to find regulations relevant to your research and to ensure that they are up-to-date.

Other Legal Research Tools

This section of the checklist encourages the use of less obvious research tools that are not found in the law library such as memoranda databases, social science research, and government directories. These resources, in appropriate circumstances, allow you to short cut your research or to access necessary and useful information which you would not otherwise find.

English and American Legal Research

American and English law, although not binding in Canada, can be highly persuasive, particularly when the Canadian law on the topic has not been well developed or when the Canadian law is in a state of confusion. Research from other foreign jurisdictions may be relevant, but for Canadian purposes, English and American research are the most prevalent.

Appendix I

RESEARCH CHECKLIST

File/Course Name _____

Date Assigned: _____ **Date Due:** _____

Description of Issues:

☐ **Canadian Encyclopedic Digest** (Chapter 4)
   C.E.D. (Ont. 3rd) and C.E.D. (West 3rd)

☐ **Treatises** (Chapter 5)
   Canadian Abridgment: Index to Canadian Legal Literature

☐ **Periodicals** (Chapter 6)
   Indexes:
      (1) Current Law Index
      (2) Index to Legal Periodicals
      (3) Index to Canadian Legal Periodical Literature
      (4) Canadian Abridgment: Index to Canadian Legal Literature
      (5) Legal Journals Index
      (6) Index to Foreign Legal Periodicals
      (7) Index to Periodicals Related to Law

☐ **Conference and Seminar Materials** (Chapter 7)
   Canadian Abridgment: Index to Canadian Legal Literature

☐ **Law Reform Commission Reports** (Chapter 8)
   Canadian Abridgment: Index to Canadian Legal Literature

☐ **Looseleaf Services** (Chapter 9)
      (1) "Living Texts"
      (2) Consolidated Statutes and Regulations
      (3) Annotated Statutes
      (4) Court Forms and Precedents

☐ **Topical Law Reports** (Chapter 10)
Cumulative Index updated by subsequent Volumes

☐ **Canadian Abridgment** (Chapter 11)
   (1) Case Digests
   (2) Canadian Case Citations
   (3) Canadian Citations: Statutes Judicially Considered
   (4) Canadian Citations: Rules Judicially Considered
   (5) Words & Phrases
   (6) Consolidated Table of Cases
   (7) Index to Canadian Legal Literature

☐ **Unreported Decisions** (Chapter 12)
   (1) Legal Database Systems
   (2) Commercial Digest Services

☐ **Noting Up Cases** (Chapter 11)
Use Canadian Case Citations portion of the Canadian Abridgment
and Computer Database

☐ **Legal Dictionaries (Words & Phrases)** (Chapter 13)
   (1) Canadian Abridgment
   (2) Sanagan's Encyclopedia of Words and Phrases, Legal Maxims, Canada 1825 to 1985
   (3) Carswell Topical Report Services
   (4) Yogis, A Canadian Law Dictionary
   (5) Black's Law Dictionary

☐ **Constitutional Research** (Chapter 14)

☐ **Statutory Research** (Chapter 15)
Update
Check for Judicial Consideration using Canadian Citations:
Statutes Judicially Considered portion of the Canadian
Abridgment

☐ **Regulatory Research** (Chapter 16)
Update

☐ **Other Legal Research Tools** (Chapter 17)
   (1) Government Telephone Directories
   (2) Databases of Memoranda of Law
   (3) Legal Publishers' Mailing Lists
   (4) Social Science Research
   (5) Specialized Industrial Relations Periodicals
   (6) Press Reports
   (7) Martindale-Hubbell Law Directory

☐ **English Legal Research** (Chapter 18)

☐ **American Legal Research** (Chapter 19)

4

Canadian Encyclopedic Digest

WHAT IS THE CANADIAN ENCYCLOPEDIC DIGEST?

The *Canadian Encyclopedic Digest* ("*C.E.D.*") is a looseleaf multi-volume legal encyclopedia which provides a broad narrative of the law. Since the *C.E.D.* is published in looseleaf binders, new legal developments can be inserted on a regular basis. The Ontario *C.E.D.* (cited, *C.E.D. (Ont.* 3rd)), focuses on Ontario and federal laws, whereas the Western C.E.D. (cited, *C.E.D. (West* 3rd)), focuses on the law in the Western provinces and the two territories and federal laws. Both the *C.E.D. (Ont.* 3rd) and the *C.E.D. (West* 3rd) cite decisions from other common law provinces, Britain, and other common law jurisdictions where appropriate.

WHEN IS THE C.E.D. USEFUL?

We recommend beginning your research by consulting the *C.E.D.*, particularly if you are unfamiliar with the topic you have been asked to research. The *C.E.D.* will provide you with an overview of the law before you delve into subtleties. Accordingly, you should not expect to find a detailed discussion of a particular case or statutory provision. In addition, you should not rely on the *C.E.D.* to refer you to all the relevant law on your topic. The *C.E.D.* is not as thorough as a treatise and should not be used as a substitute for a treatise.

While it is appropriate to cite a treatise in a legal memorandum or law school essay, you should not cite the *C.E.D.*.

HOW IS THE C.E.D. ORGANIZED?

The *C.E.D.* consists of approximately thirty-eight looseleaf binders organized alphabetically by subject titles. There are roughly one hundred and fifty-nine subject titles, each covering a broad area of law such as contracts, evidence, and family law, or a specific area of law, such as boundaries, fines, and prisons.

The text of the *C.E.D.* is organized by paragraph numbers. Each paragraph contains statements of law which are substantiated by cases and statutory provisions referenced in footnotes. The *C.E.D.* titles contain a "Table of Cases", a "Table of Statutes" and individual subject indexes.

These tables will refer you to the place in the text where the case or statutory provision is cited.

An Index Binder or "Key" facilitates easy access to the subject binders. This binder contains:

A *"Contents Key"* reproducing the table of contents in each of the main volumes of the C.E.D. The volume in which the subject titles can be found is indicated.

A *"Statutes Key"* listing in alphabetical order the statutes referred to in the various subject titles with references to the volume and paragraph numbers where the statutes or provisions thereof are discussed.

A *"Rules and Regulations Key"* listing in alphabetical order the rules and regulations referred to in the subject titles with references to volume and paragraph numbers.

A *"Key-Words Index"* indicating the volume(s) and the volume and paragraph numbers where the "words" (denoting subtopics), listed alphabetically, are discussed.

There is also an index behind each title in the subject binders of the *C.E.D.* You can refer directly to these indexes if you know what subject title to look under. However, these indexes will only refer you to the appropriate paragraph numbers for the subject title under which you are looking. In contrast, the Key-Words Index in the Key Binder will refer you, where applicable, to paragraph numbers in a variety of subject titles.

The *C.E.D.* is updated approximately once a year. A "Recent Developments" section is found in the front section of most titles and is denoted by yellow supplementary pages. The paragraph numbers in the "Recent Developments" section correspond to the paragraph numbers in the main body of the text. If the paragraph number you have been researching in the main body of the text does not appear in the "Recent Developments" section, there have been no changes in the law up to the time the *C.E.D.* was last updated.

The information in the main body of the *C.E.D.* is accurate, at minimum, as of the date on the bottom of the page in which you are researching. The information in the "Recent Developments" section is accurate, at minimum, as of the date on the bottom of the page in which you are researching in this section.

HOW TO USE THE C.E.D.

1.   Consult the Index Binder under your topic. The "Key-Words Index" will normally be the most useful, particularly if you are unsure under which title(s) your subtopic falls. You will be

referred to both title number(s) and paragraph numbers in the subject binders. In using the Index, try to be creative and persistent. An area of law about which you know nothing may use unusual terminology. Be sure to try several approaches before concluding that the *C.E.D.* has nothing on your issue.

2. Consult the Index at the back of the Title to which you have been referred for a further breakdown of key words or phrases.

3. Refer to the appropriate paragraph numbers under your title(s). You are now up-to-date, at minimum, as of the date at the bottom of the page on which you are researching.

4. Update by referring to the "Recent Developments" section, the coloured pages at the front of the section in which you are researching. Look for the paragraph numbers in the "Recent Developments" section which correspond to the paragraphs you are researching in the main body of the text. You are now up-to-date, at minimum, as of the date on the bottom of the page in which you are researching. If the relevant paragraph numbers do not appear in the "Recent Developments" section, there have been no changes in the law as of the date up to which the *C.E.D.* was last updated.

USING THE C.E.D. IN CONJUNCTION WITH THE ABRIDGMENT

Always note up cases cited in the *C.E.D.* using the *Canadian Case Citations* portion of the *Canadian Abridgment*.[1] Although the *C.E.D.* will tell you if a case has been overturned, as of the date in which the *C.E.D.* was last updated, it will not tell you how the case has been subsequently applied, distinguished, or interpreted. A detailed examination of the subsequent judicial consideration of the cases on which you are relying can be vital to your research.

---

1 See Chapter Eleven on how to use the *Canadian Case Citations* portion of the *Canadian Abridgment*.

5

Treatises

WHAT IS A TREATISE?

A treatise is a text on an area of law. It is useful to distinguish treatises from casebooks. Casebooks contain excerpts of cases in a given area of law. The authors of casebooks may add some editorial commentary, but do not offer a detailed interpretive guide to the law. Treatises provide an in depth narrative and interpretation of the law.

Treatises can be persuasive sources of secondary legal literature, depending on the author and the quality of the book, and are frequently cited or quoted in judicial decisions.

WHEN IS A TREATISE USEFUL?

After you have consulted a legal encyclopedia to obtain a broad overview of your topic (assuming that you require such an overview), we recommend checking to see if there is a treatise on your subject area. Treatises will provide a more in depth treatment of your subject than a legal encyclopedia. A treatise will direct you to many of the relevant cases on your subject and provide an interpretive guide to these cases. Treatises will also alert you to any peculiarities of a certain area of law.

A treatise is, however, only a starting point. Never assume that the author of a treatise has cited all of the relevant case law on your subject. While the author may have cited many of the important cases, it is highly unlikely that the author will have dealt with all cases. Accordingly, there may be case law which is relevant to your research problem but is not cited in the treatise. You should also always read the cases cited in a treatise. Never rely on an author's interpretation of a case without reading it yourself.

HOW TO USE A TREATISE

1. Check the list of treatises in the selective topical bibliography at Chapter Twenty-one and the card catalogues or computer data base of your law library to see if there is a treatise on your topic. The *Canadian Abridgment: Index to Canadian Legal Literature* also indexes treatises.[1]

---

1 For an explanation on how to use the *Canadian Abridgment: Index to Canadian Legal Literature* see Chapter Eleven.

2.   When you have found the treatise, scan the table of contents and index for your subject area. Be sensitive to the peculiarities of the terminology of your subject. Your topic may be indexed under something unexpected.

3.   Turn to the relevant chapter or page of the treatise for an overview of the law and make a note of the relevant cases cited.

USING TREATISES IN CONJUNCTION WITH THE ABRIDGMENT

Always note up cases cited in the treatise on which you are relying using the *Canadian Case Citations* portion of the *Canadian Abridgment*.[2] Although a treatise will tell you if a case has been overturned, as of the date in which the treatise is current, it will not tell you how the case has been subsequently applied, distinguished, or interpreted. A detailed examination of the subsequent judicial consideration of the cases on which you are relying on can be vital to your research.

---

2 See Chapter Eleven on how to use the *Canadian Case Citations* portion of the *Canadian Abridgment*.

6

Legal Periodicals

WHAT ARE PERIODICALS?

Legal periodicals or journals publish articles, case comments, and book reviews on various areas of the law. There are two types of periodicals: (*a*) general periodicals which publish articles on all areas of law; and (*b*) topical periodicals which publish articles on specific areas of the law only. Periodicals can be persuasive sources of secondary legal literature depending on the thoroughness and quality of the author's analysis.

WHEN ARE PERIODICALS USEFUL?

Periodicals are particularly useful when you are researching a new field of law or a field which has just undergone changes or developments. Periodicals are published more frequently than treatises, and thus often provide more current information. Periodical articles also tend to be more focused than treatises. A treatise, for instance, may provide an overview of the entire law of contracts; a periodical article, on the other hand, will likely focus on a discrete area of contract law. For this reason, if you are unfamiliar with the area of law, we recommend first looking at a legal encyclopedia or treatise to get an overview and then consulting periodical articles. Case comments of significant decisions are also useful.[1]

Case comments show how a decision has affected the law and, therefore, often contain an overview of the law on the topic. It is useful to look for case comments once you have found the relevant case law on your topic. You will tend to find case comments on decisions that are contentious or have made a significant contribution to the law.

Never assume that an article or case comment has cited all of the relevant law on your topic and always read the case law for yourself to ensure that your interpretation corresponds with the author's. The researcher should be aware that journal articles are often written from a certain political or theoretical perspective.

HOW ARE PERIODICALS INDEXED?

Periodical indexes facilitate quick access to journal articles, case comments, and book reviews. There are different volumes for different

---

1 See Chapter Twenty for a discussion of the mechanics of writing a case comment.

years. Materials are indexed as follows: articles according to subject; articles according to author; case comments according to case name; case comments according to subject; and book reviews according to author and/or title of the book.

There are seven main periodical indexes:

1. *Current Law Index*;
2. *Index to Legal Periodicals*;
3. *Index to Canadian Legal Periodical Literature*;
4. *Canadian Abridgment: Index to Canadian Legal Literature*;
5. *Legal Journals Index*;
6. *Index to Foreign Legal Periodicals*; and
7. *Index to Periodical Articles Related to Law*.

Current Law Index is the most comprehensive periodical index. It covers over 700 periodicals published in the Commonwealth and the United States. If you are doing in depth research on a topic and require foreign legal analysis, Current Law Index is your best choice. We would recommend using this index in most instances, particularly if you are interested in Canadian and foreign periodical literature.

Index to Legal Periodicals covers over 400 legal journals from Canada, the United States, England, Ireland, Australia, and New Zealand.

Index to Canadian Legal Periodical Literature covers Canadian journals only. Although this is the least comprehensive of the above indexes, if you are looking for Canadian articles and/or case comments only, it is sufficiently thorough.

Canadian Abridgment: Index to Canadian Legal Literature is broader than the *Index to Canadian Legal Periodical Literature* in that it does not restrict itself to indexing periodicals. In addition to periodicals, the following forms of secondary legal literature are indexed: treatises, academic publications (casebooks, theses), essays from edited collections, government publications, law society and bar association publications, continuing legal education materials, and audio-visual materials. If you need to find secondary literature other than periodicals, you should consult the *Canadian Abridgment: Index to Canadian Legal Literature*.[2]

Legal Journals Index covers all legal journals published in the United Kingdom.

Index to Foreign Legal Periodicals covers articles dealing with international and comparative law in addition to the law of common law countries excluding Canada, the United Kingdom, and the United States.

---

2 For an explanation of how to use the *Canadian Abridgment: Index to Canadian Legal Literature* see Chapter Eleven. The explanation of how to use periodical indexes below does not apply to this index.

Index to Periodicals Related to Law covers articles published throughout the English-speaking world on social science, scientific, and medical topics with legal dimensions.

HOW TO FIND PERIODICAL ARTICLES

1. Refer to one of the above periodical indexes for each year in which you require literature.
2. Skim through the section on Subject Headings which you will find at the beginning of each volume. Review the headings carefully, as an article may not always be indexed under the heading which appears most obvious to you.
3. Refer to the appropriate subject headings where you will find a list of articles with citations.
4. The citation of the journal will be an abbreviation. If you do not understand what the abbreviation means, refer to the front of the index where you will find a list of all the journals covered in the volume with their abbreviations.

HOW TO FIND CASE COMMENTS

When you know the Case Name

1. Refer to one of the above periodical indexes for the year in which the case was decided and the year after the case was decided. Most case comments are written shortly after a case is decided.
2. Look up the case name in the Table of Cases. If a case comment has been published, you will find it listed here with a citation.

When you know the Subject but not the Case Name

1. Skim through the section on Subject Headings which you will find at the beginning of each volume. Review the headings carefully, as a case comment may not always be indexed under the heading which appears most obvious to you.
2. Refer to the appropriate Subject Headings. If there has been a case comment, it will be listed after the articles on the subject.

COMMENTARY ON SUPREME COURT OF CANADA DECISIONS

When your research involves a topic where there has been Supreme Court of Canada jurisprudence, it is a good idea to check if there has been a case comment or article on point. The *Supreme Court Law Review* is a particularly useful periodical. It is an annual publication of articles on developments in various areas of law as a result of recent Supreme Court of Canada jurisprudence. The areas of law covered are: administrative law; constitutional law; criminal law and procedure; contracts and torts; droit civil; evidence; employment; property; and leave to appeal applications: (i) criminal, (ii) civil, and (iii) administrative.

7

Conference and Seminar Materials

WHAT ARE CONFERENCE AND SEMINAR MATERIALS?

A number of organizations offer conferences and seminars for members of the legal profession and/or industry. These conferences generally include written material that summarizes and supplements the oral presentations.

WHEN ARE CONFERENCE AND SEMINAR MATERIALS USEFUL?

Papers from conferences and seminars, like journal articles, may save the researcher time by providing a summary of the law in the area or topic. Conference and seminar materials tend to have a very practical focus. They also tend to highlight recent developments in the law and their implications. You will often find recent seminar materials to be more up-to-date than journal articles due to the publication lag with respect to journals.

The usual caveat respecting the use of secondary sources applies — any references to statutes or cases should be verified.

HOW TO FIND CONFERENCE AND SEMINAR MATERIALS

The various organizations that offer seminars and conferences publish catalogues and indexes of past seminars. The material usually can be accessed by subject or author. Seminar and conference materials are also indexed under subject headings in the *Canadian Abridgment: Index to Canadian Legal Literature* portion.[1]

---

1 See Chapter Eleven on the *Canadian Abridgment* on how to use this research tool.

8

Law Reform Commission Reports

WHAT ARE LAW REFORM COMMISSION REPORTS?

Law reform commissions are independent legal think-tanks which study and publish reports on legal reform. The reports typically begin by outlining what the law is on a given topic (for instance, the law on drug and alcohol testing in the workplace). Next, they demonstrate why the law or procedure being studied should be reformed. Finally, they make concrete recommendations to government on how the law could be reformed. In developing these recommendations, they often examine the laws and/or procedures of other jurisdictions.

Law reform commission reports are regarded as highly persuasive secondary authorities. They are frequently quoted in judicial decisions and often form the basis of legislative reform.

The federal law reform commission was discontinued in 1992. However, most provinces have their own law reform commissions.

WHEN ARE LAW REFORM COMMISSION REPORTS USEFUL?

Law reform commission reports can be used to obtain an overview of selected legal and procedural topics, since they outline what the law is, before discussing suggested reforms. Like periodicals, law reform commission reports are particularly useful when researching new fields of law (or new areas within a well-developed field). Often when researching a new field of law, you will not find a treatise on your topic and a looseleaf service may only have a few sentences or paragraphs on point; however, you may find an entire law reform commission report which deals exclusively with your topic.

Law reform commission reports are also very useful when your research requires you to analyze and comment not only on what the law is but also on what it could and should be.

As with other secondary legal literature, never assume that a law reform commission report has cited all of the case law on your topic and always read the case law for yourself to ensure that your interpretation corresponds with the commission's.

HOW TO FIND LAW REFORM COMMISSION REPORTS

You will find many or all law reform commission reports in your law library, indexed by subject or author (i.e., Ontario Law Reform Commission). The *Canadian Abridgment: Index to Canadian Legal Literature* also indexes law reform commission reports.[1] Finally, you can write to the law reform commission in your province for a list of commission reports and order such reports directly from the commission.[2]

---

1   For an explanation of how to use the *Canadian Abridgment: Index to Canadian Legal Literature* consult Chapter Eleven.

2   In Ontario, copies of law reform commission reports that are still in print can be ordered from: Publications Services, Ministry of Government Services, 5th Floor, 880 Bay Street, Toronto, Ontario, Canada M7A 1N8, Telephone (416) 326-5300.

British Columbia Law Reform working papers can be ordered from: the Commission, 601-865 Hornby Street, Vancouver, British Columbia, Canada V6Z 2G3, Telephone (604) 660-2366.

British Columbia Law Reform Commission Reports can be ordered from: Crown Publications, 546 Yates Street, Victoria, British Columbia, Canada V8W 1K8, Telephone (604) 386-4636.

Nova Scotia Law Reform Commission Reports can be obtained from: the Nova Scotia Law Reform Commission, 8th Floor, Garrison Place, 1526 Dresden Row, Halifax, Nova Scotia, Canada B3J 2K2, Telephone (902) 423-2633.

9

Looseleaf Services

WHAT IS A LOOSELEAF SERVICE?

Looseleaf services are published in binders so that new developments in the law can be inserted regularly and obsolete law removed. These services can therefore save the researcher a tremendous amount of time and effort updating the law.

There are four main types of looseleaf services:

(a) legal encyclopedias and other works which summarize the law in a particular area ("living texts");

(b) consolidated versions of a statute and regulations;

(c) annotated statutes; and

(d) court forms and precedents.

Looseleaf services which are *living texts* may provide a broad overview of the law (e.g., the *C.E.D.*) or a detailed analysis and interpretive guide of a specific area of the law (e.g., *The Mercer Pension Manual*). Many texts which were initially published in bound volumes are being reprinted in a looseleaf form so that recent developments in the law can be inserted without the necessity of waiting for another bound volume to come out. For instance, the third edition of Hogg's *Constitutional Law of Canada* is in looseleaf form.

A *looseleaf version of a statute or regulations* will save the researcher time in the updating process. Where a looseleaf version of a statute exists, it will not be necessary to refer to the bound sessional volumes, nor will it be necessary to check all editions of the *Gazette*.

A looseleaf version of the statute or regulation that is *annotated* will include commentary, citations and/or summaries of the cases which have interpreted the provisions of the statute. Annotated statutes may save having to check the *Canadian Case Citations* portion of the *Canadian Abridgment* (the "*Abridgment*"). However, the researcher should be aware that many annotated statutes do not cite all cases which have interpreted the provisions of the statute. Instead, some of the more important cases are selected under each section of the statute. Therefore, depending on the depth of your research, it may still be necessary to consult *Canadian Case Citations*.

The final category of looseleaf service is a compilation of *forms or precedents* to assist in legal drafting. An example is *Williston & Rolls Court Forms (Toronto: Butterworths)*, which is a four volume set that contains the forms used at every stage of a civil action and offers detailed guidance in the preparation of these forms. The sequence and format of the material covered in this looseleaf accords with the sequence and format of the *Rules of Civil Procedure.*

Other valuable looseleafs exist which fall less neatly into the four categories outlined above. For instance, there are two excellent looseleaf services on limitation periods, both by Crisp, Ditta and Joffe, *Federal Limitation Periods* and *Ontario Limitation Periods* (Toronto: Butterworths), which list all limitation periods under federal and Ontario statutes, respectively. The limitation periods are listed according to both statute name and subject. These looseleafs are very time-saving, particularly when the researcher does not know under which statute the relevant limitation period falls.

WHEN ARE LOOSELEAF SERVICES USEFUL?

A looseleaf service will save the researcher a significant amount of time in the updating of the law process. Therefore, if a looseleaf service exists in your subject area, you should consult it at a preliminary stage of your research so that you do not increase your work by collecting information that a looseleaf service has already compiled.

HOW TO USE A LOOSELEAF SERVICE

All looseleaf services are different so it is best to begin by reading the instructions in the first volume of the looseleaf service you are using at the time. When reading the instructions, there are two vital pieces of information you will want to obtain:

(*a*) how to access the information you need; and
(*b*) how to determine whether the information you have accessed is up-to-date.

Generally you will be able to access the information you require by looking in the table of contents or index of the looseleaf.

To determine to what extent the information you have accessed is current, check the date on the page that you are researching. The information will be accurate, at minimum, as of that date. The front page of the looseleaf service may also indicate when the looseleaf was last updated.

Some looseleafs — usually those which summarize the law — have a section in the front entitled "Recent Developments". Often this section is denoted by pages of a different colour. Always check whether there have been any new developments in the law you are researching by checking under this section.

Generally the titles or headings used in the main body of the looseleaf will correspond to the titles used in the "Recent Developments" section. In this case, simply look for the title you are researching in the main body of the looseleaf. If the title does not appear in the "Recent Developments" section, there have been no new developments as of the date on which the looseleaf was last updated.

Sometimes titles or headings are not used in the "Recent Developments" section. Instead, paragraph numbers which correspond to the paragraphs in the main body of the text will be used. Look for the paragraph numbers in the "Recent Developments" section which correspond with the paragraphs you are researching in the main body of the text. If the relevant paragraph numbers do not appear in the "Recent Developments" section, there have been no changes in the law as of the date on which the looseleaf was last updated.

COMMERCE CLEARING HOUSE ("C.C.H.") LOOSELEAFS: AN ILLUSTRATION

C.C.H. Canada Limited publishes over 50 topical looseleafs.

How to Determine if a C.C.H. Looseleaf Exists in the Area You are Researching?

Consult the current edition of the C.C.H. Rapid Finder Index to determine whether there is a looseleaf for the area of law you are researching. The Rapid Finder Index is a paperback yearly publication (available without charge from C.C.H. Canada) that lists the main subjects covered in the looseleafs. Subjects are listed alphabetically, followed by the titles of the looseleafs in which information on the subject is published. For instance, if you were researching disability benefits, the Rapid Finder Index would direct you to the following C.C.H. looseleafs:

Disability Benefits

— Canadian Employment Benefits and Pension Guide
— Canadian Employment Safety and Health Guide
— Canadian Labour Law Reports
— Canadian Payroll Management Guide

How are C.C.H. Looseleafs Indexed?

C.C.H. looseleafs are indexed in three ways:
(*a*) by Subject;

(*b*)   by Case Name; and

(*c*)   by Number.

Subject

You will typically select the first method of accessing information. Consult the topical index of the looseleaf under the subject you are researching. The topical index includes main headings and sub-headings. After each heading or sub-heading, the index will refer you to the paragraph number(s) in the looseleaf dealing with the topic.

Case Name

If you have a case name and wish to locate information relating to the case, consult the Table of Cases in the looseleaf which covers the subject of the case. The Table of Cases provides the paragraph where the decision is discussed or cited in the looseleaf. Decisions are listed in alphabetical order.

Number

If you have a numerical reference to a statute, regulation or bulletin, you can consult the Finding Lists. Finding Lists translate the section numbers of statutes or regulations into paragraph numbers.

Use of Paragraph Numbers

References throughout C.C.H. looseleafs are to paragraph numbers, not page numbers. Paragraph numbers are preceded by a paragraph sign and enclosed in square brackets. Page numbers will appear at the top of each page. However page numbers are only used for the purpose of filing current inserts of the looseleaf.

How are C.C.H. Looseleafs Updated?

New or amending laws or regulations are generally reported by the replacement and addition of affected pages.

Proposed legislation or new court decisions are found in a separate "New Matters" section of the looseleaf. The paragraph numbers in the "New Matters" section correspond to the paragraph numbers in the main body of the looseleaf. Therefore look for the paragraph numbers in the "New Matters" section which correspond with the paragraphs you are researching in the main body of the looseleaf. If the relevant paragraph numbers do not appear in the "New Matters" section, there have been no changes in the law as of the date on which the looseleaf was last updated.

10

Law Reports

WHAT ARE LAW REPORTS?

Law reports are regularly issued volumes that contain the written reasons for judgment of cases.

Law reports can be classified as either "*official reports*" or "*unofficial reports*". Official reports are published pursuant to a statute by an official government printer. The statute is generally one that provides for the creation of the court whose decisions the report publishes. The Supreme Court of Canada and the Federal Court of Canada both have an official report: *Canada Supreme Court Reports* (S.C.R.) and *Canada Federal Court Reports* (F.C.). There are no official provincial report series.

Unofficial reports are published under the authority of a statutorily created regulatory body or a private organization (commercial publisher). Sometimes a case will be cited in both official and unofficial reports.

The distinction between official and unofficial reports only becomes relevant when you are writing a factum for either the Federal Court or the Supreme Court of Canada. In Federal Court or Supreme Court of Canada facta, the official report must be cited and included in your book of authorities whenever the case is reported in an official report.

Law reports can also be categorized by the type of decision they report:

Judicial Origin Reports: Report cases from a particular court or courts. Examples include the *Supreme Court Reports* (report cases from the Supreme Court of Canada only); the *Federal Court of Canada Reports* (report all cases from the Federal Court of Appeal and selected cases from the Federal Court Trial Division); and the *National Reporter* (report all cases from the Supreme Court of Canada and the Federal Court of Appeal and selected cases from the Federal Court Trial Division).

Cross-Canada Reports: Report cases decided at all court levels in all Canadian jurisdictions. The *Dominion Law Reports* are Canada's national law reports.

Regional Reports: Report cases decided at all court levels in a particular region of the country. There are two regional law reports, the *Atlantic Provinces Reports* (covers new Brunswick, Newfoundland, Nova Scotia, and Prince Edward Island) and the *Western Weekly*

Reports (covers Alberta, Saskatchewan, Manitoba, and British Columbia).

Provincial Reports: Report cases decided at all court levels within a province or territory. Examples include the *Ontario Reports*, and the *North West Territories Reports*. Every province has its own law report series.

Topical Reports: Report cases decided on a particular subject.[1] Examples include *Canadian Bankruptcy Reports, Canadian Environmental Law Reports*, and *Reports of Family Law*.

Reports of Decisions of Administrative Tribunals: These reports tend to be *de facto* subject reports since administrative tribunals have jurisdiction over defined subject areas. Some of the reports of administrative tribunals, in addition to publishing the decisions of the tribunal, also publish judicial decisions arising in the subject-area. Examples include *Canadian Labour Relations Board Reports, Immigration Appeal Cases*, and *Ontario Human Rights Commission Reports*.

HOW ARE LAW REPORTS ORGANIZED?

Law reports are organized in volumes which cover cases over a given time period. Many law reports have several series. For instance, the *Dominion Law Reports* currently has four series: the "old" first series (1912-1922); the "new" first series (1923-1955); the second series (1956-1968); the third series (1969-1984); and the fourth series (1984 to present).

Law reports generally contain in each volume — a table of cases and a subject index of cases cited in that particular volume or law report. A synopsis or headnote of the cases listed under each subject heading is also generally included. Use of these features saves having to look up cases which, although under your subject heading, are irrelevant to your research needs.

Consolidated or cumulative indexes are published at intervals. They index decisions in a series of volumes so that you do not have to refer to the index in every volume of the series.

The cumulative index of topical law reports published by Carswell also index:

- statutes judicially considered
- rules judicially considered
- regulations judicially considered
- forms judicially considered
- authorities judicially considered

---

1 See Selective Topical Bibliography for topical law reports on various topics.

- words and phrases judicially considered
- annotations of articles by subject
- annotations of articles by author

These research features can save having to use the *Canadian Abridgment* (the *"Abridgment"*) to find statutes, rules, and words and phrases that have been judicially considered. However, since topical law reports only report cases on a particular subject, the cumulative index of a topical law report series will not refer you to statutes, rules, and words and phrases, as they have been considered in other fields of law. Therefore, depending on the scope of your research, you may have to consult other sources as well.

WHEN ARE REPORT SERIES USEFUL FOR RESEARCH PURPOSES?

Law Reports can be used for research purposes to obtain cases on a particular subject or to obtain the citation of a case digested in a report series. You should never rely solely on the *Canadian Encyclopedic Digest*, a treatise, or a journal article to find all the relevant cases on your subject. The topical reports published by Carswell also can be used to research statutes, regulations, rules, forms, authorities, and words and phrases that have been judicially considered.

When a topical law report exists for your subject, we recommend using it over the *Abridgment* to find cases on your subject.[2] Topical Reports permit more time-efficient research than the *Abridgment*.

The subject index of the *Dominion Law Reports*, which is Canada's national law reports, is also a useful tool for locating cases on a given topic. However, if a topical law report series exists on your subject, it is preferable to use it over the *Dominion Law Reports*. As topical law reports only publish cases on a given subject, they permit more thorough research on that subject.

We do not recommend using regional, provincial, or judicial origin reports to find cases on a particular subject *unless* you are only looking for cases in the region or province that the report covers or in the level of court that the report covers.

HOW TO USE A LAW REPORT

Finding Cases on a Subject

1. Consult the consolidated or cumulative index under your subject or other heading.

---

2 See Selective Topical Bibliography for a list of topical reporters.

2. Consult each report series subsequent to the consolidated or cumulative index under your subject heading.
3. Locate the relevant cases in the appropriate volumes of the report series.

Locating a Case When You do not Know the Citation but You do Know that the Case is Reported in a Particular Series[3]

1. Consult the Table of Cases in the consolidated or cumulative Index.
2. Consult the Table of Cases in each report series not digested in the consolidated or cumulative index under your subject heading.
3. Locate the case in the appropriate volume of the report series.

---

3 If you know only the name of a case or you wish to see if it was reported in another report series, check the *Consolidated Table of Cases* portion of the *Canadian Abridgment* which is discussed in Chapter Eleven.

11

Canadian Abridgment

WHAT IS THE CANADIAN ABRIDGMENT?

The *Canadian Abridgment* (the *"Abridgment"*) is the most comprehensive Canadian legal research tool, and mastery of it is absolutely essential. The sections of the *Abridgment* and how to use them are outlined in this chapter. The *Abridgment* allows you to research:

Case Law relating to a specific legal issue: Collect cases from a wide array of Canadian courts and tribunals in a given subject area;

History and judicial teatment of a Case ("Noting Up"): Trace the subsequent judicial consideration of a given case;

History and judicial treatment of Statutes and Rules of Practice: Collect cases that have considered a statute, a section of a statute or a rule of practice;

Judicial Interpretation of Words and Phrases: Collect cases that have discussed the interpretation of a word or phrase;

All available citations for a case: Find all of the citations for a case if you have the name of the case; and

Legal Literature: Find books, journal or periodical articles, case comments, annotations, academic publications, essays from edited collections, federal and provincial government publications, continuing legal education materials, and public legal education materials on a given subject or by a given author.

HOW IS THE ABRIDGMENT ORGANIZED?

The *Abridgment* has different sections that correspond to the different functions that it performs.

Case Digests

There is a *Key & Research Guide* binder that contains various indexing tools for accessing the case digests by subject area in the *Abridgment*. Case digests are summaries of cases that contain relevant legal details. By reviewing the digests you should be able to select those cases that answer your research problem.

The case digests are contained in a permanent set of volumes containing a comprehensive collection of case digests (summaries of cases) organized by subject-area. Each of these volumes is updated by a softcover Supplement volume. The Supplement volumes, as their name suggests, supplement the main volumes of the *Abridgment*. The Supplement volumes are further updated by periodically issued softcover editions of *Canadian Current Law: Case Law Digests*.

The *Abridgment* tries to be comprehensive, and contains cases from all Canadian courts and many tribunals. All reported decisions should be contained in the *Abridgment* and quite a few unreported decisions are included as well. Since 1987 all unreported cases decided by the Courts of Appeal across Canada have been included.

NOTE: Quebec civil law decisions are not covered by the *Abridgment*.

The current permanent volume collection of the *Abridgment* is known as the "Revised Second Edition". Revised Second Edition main volumes can be identified by a capital "R" which appears on the cover; for example "R1" is volume one of the Revised Second Edition. Permanent volumes are further supplemented by permanent supplement volumes. They can be identified by the word "Supplement" following the volume number; for example "R1 Supplement" is the volume that supplements "R1".

The subjects themselves are organized according to the Key Classification System which breaks a subject area down into increasingly more specific levels, using first Roman numerals, then arabic numerals, and then letters. For example, "PRACTICE" is a subject area and PRACTICE III 2d is:

    III   Institution of Proceedings
        2.   Writ of Summons
           d.   Insurance

Each case digest is given a Key Classification Number.

Canadian Case Citations

The *Abridgment* provides two methods of finding the judicial treatment of cases or "noting up". Originally a series of volumes, entitled *Cases Judicially Considered*, were issued that allowed the user to trace the history of a case as it has been judicially considered — that is, whether the case has been followed, overruled, discussed, etc. Cases in these volumes are arranged alphabetically by name in a series of bound volumes that are arranged in chronological order, with each volume covering a different time period. In 1986, the publisher changed the name of these volumes to *Canadian Citations: Cases Judicially Considered*. Then in 1991, the publisher decided to simplify the system, by issuing a set of volumes known as *Canadian Case Citations 1867-1990*. These volumes replace all of the earlier *Cases Judicially Considered* volumes, meaning that if you have access to the *Canadian Case Citations 1867-1990* set, you can look up the name of the case once as opposed to working your way through all of the successive volumes in the old system. Cases are organized alphabetically by name. If you only have access to the old system volumes, you can still use them. Both the new and the old system volumes are further updated by annually issued volumes titled *Canadian Case Citations*, a softcover quarterly supplement, and finally by softcover monthly issues of *Canadian Case Citations*.

NOTE: Canadian judicial consideration of foreign cases can be found in this part of the *Abridgment*. It is therefore possible to "note-up" foreign cases which have been considered by Canadian courts.

Judicial Consideration of Statutes and Rules of Practice

The *Abridgment* contains a series of volumes that allow the user to collect the judicial considerations of a statute, section of a statute, or of a rule of practice. Included are international treaties and conventions, foreign statutes, and Canadian federal, provincial, and territorial statutes. Statutes are organized alphabetically under the headings of international treaties and conventions, Canadian federal statutes, each province, or territory. United Kingdom statutes are arranged chronologically.

The bound volumes are arranged in chronological order covering successive time periods. Older volumes are titled *Statutes Judicially Considered*. In 1986, the "Rules of Practice" feature was added, and in 1987 the title was changed to *Canadian Citations: Statutes Judicially Considered/Rules Judicially Considered*. The bound volumes are further updated by a softcover quarterly supplement, and finally by monthly issues of *Canadian Citations: Statutes Judicially Considered*.

Judicial Interpretation of Words & Phrases

The *Abridgment* has a bound volume "Words & Phrases Revised" in which there is an alphabetical list of words and phrases that have been judicially considered. Under a given word or phrase are listed the cases with their citations, in which the word or phrase was considered. The bound volume is updated by the "Words & Phrases" portion in the *General Index* binder, which is further updated by the "Words & Phrases" section in *Canadian Current Law: Case Law Digests*.

All Available Citations for a Case

The *Abridgment* has a set of looseleaf binders known as the *Consolidated Table of Cases*. Cases are organized alphabetically by name in the binders. There are yellow pages and white pages for each letter. The yellow pages update the contents of each binder appearing on the white pages.

Legal Literature

The *Abridgment* has a set of chronologically ordered volumes titled the *Index to Canadian Legal Literature*. A new bound volume is issued every year. The bound volumes are further updated by periodically issued editions of *Canadian Current Law: Canadian Legal Literature*. Materials can be accessed by:

- subject
- author
- case name
- statute (and section number)

There is also a book review index that provides access to reviews by:

- author of book
- title of book
- author of review

All Canadian secondary legal literature may be accessed, including:

- treatises
- articles
- case comments
- annotations
- academic publications (casebooks, theses)
- essays from edited collections
- government publications
- law society/bar association publications
- continuing legal education materials
- public education materials
- audio-visual materials

HOW TO USE THE VARIOUS SECTIONS OF THE ABRIDGMENT [1]

Case Digests

1. Begin by considering what is the general area of the law in which your research problem lies. You now have four alternatives:

    (*a*) You may go directly to the permanent volume that contains that area of the law. The areas of the law covered by each volume are indicated on the spines of the volumes. Once you find the subject

---

1 Carswell, the publisher of the *Abridgment*, has a toll-free helpline for users of the *Abridgment*. Toronto: (416) 298-5140. Outside Toronto: 1-800-463-4106. Hours: Monday – Thursday 9:00 a.m. to 8:00 p.m. Eastern Time, Friday 9:00 a.m. – 5:00 p.m. Eastern Time.

area in the volume, you can check the Table of Classification at the front of each subject area which outlines the Key Classification System;

(b) You may go to the Key in the *Key & Research Guide* binder which is an alphabetical list of the legal subjects and classification of the Key Classification System. You will be directed to the correct permanent volume. The Binder also contains the *Abridgment Overview* or *Subject Titles Chart*, which may also be used;

(c) You may use the *General Index* contained in the *Index Binder*, which will also direct you to the main volume.

(d) Sometimes you are instructed to begin your research on an issue with a specific case. If you know of a case, for which you want to find the digest, you can consult the *Consolidated Table of Cases* under the case name. In addition to case citations, the volume(s) and digest number(s) of the digest(s) for that case will also be given.

The alternative chosen is a matter of taste. However, we recommend use of the Key because it is updated frequently and allows you to access the law from many "key" words.

2. Next you will have to find cases that were decided subsequent to those found in the permanent volume. Examine the supplement volume that accompanies the permanent volume.

3. Check the softcover issues of *Canadian Current Law: Case Law Digests*.

You will now be up-to-date within a few months of the present. The exact date to which you are current is the date printed on the last edition of *Canadian Current Law* that you consulted.

To be even more current do a search of a computer database. Computer search techniques are not covered in this book, because we think that hands on experience is needed for effective learning of these skills. However, you should keep in mind that such a search is the way to have the most up-to- date research.

Canadian Case Citations (How to Note Up Cases)

1. Look up the name of the case in *Canadian Case Citations 1867-1990* or work your way through the old set of volumes that begin with *Cases Judicially Considered* volumes. Check the hardcover annual *Canadian Case Citations* volumes starting in 1991. After the most recent annual volume, check the softcover quarterly supplement. Further update this supplement with the softcover issues of *Canadian Case Citations*. You will be up-to-date as of the date printed on the last softcover issue of

Canadian Case and Statute Citations that you consult. To be as up-to-date as possible, you should note up your case further by performing a computer search.

If you find your case, you will find two kinds of entries under the case name. Symbols in a "circle" denote a judicial consideration of your case in another case. Symbols in a "square" denote a subsequent decision for the same case — the outcome of the appeal of the case you are noting up.

The symbols appearing in circles that indicate the treatment your case has received in other cases are:

F — Followed (Principle of law in cited case binding)
A — Applied (Principle of law in cited case followed but not binding)
D — Distinguished (Principle of law inapplicable because of difference in facts)
R — Referred to (Cited case referred to without comment)**this symbol has been discontinued
N — Not Followed/Overruled (Cited case expressly overruled or not applied)
Q — Quebec Civil Cases (Cited cases referred to or considered in a Quebec civil case)**this symbol has been discontinued
C — Considered (Some consideration given to cited case)

The symbols appearing in squares that indicate the treatment your case has received on subsequent consideration are:

Af — Affirmed/Judicial Review Refused
Am — Amended
Ar — Additional Reasons
Rg — Reconsideration/Rehearing Granted
Rr — Reconsideration/Rehearing Refused
Rv — Reversed
La — Leave to Appeal Allowed
Lr — Leave to Appeal Refused
Rf — Referred for further consideration/clarification
Vr — Varied
St — Set Aside/Quashed

2. *Concordance* — Between the years of 1986 and 1988, the publishers of the *Abridgment* did not print the names of the cases that considered the case being noted up under the entry for that case. In order to find the names of the cases in volumes for those years you will have to use

the Concordance that was published in each of those years. This problem will only arise for those who are using the old set of volumes.

There are two sections of the Concordance. The first section covers decisions which are reported. It is organized by:
- Abbreviation of Report Series name
- Volume number
- Page number

For example suppose you were looking for 42 O.R. (2d) 52. You would look under Ontario for the Ontario Reports (O.R.). More specifically, you would look under 42 O.R. (2d). Under that heading you would find 52 denoting the page. Under the 52 you would find the name of the case.

The second section of the Concordance covers unreported decisions. They are organized by:
- Jurisdiction
- Court
- Date (Docket numbers are given if there are two or more decisions from the same court on a given date.)

If the decision is recent and unreported, you can probably obtain a copy from a computer database. If the case is a bit older, be sure to check the *Consolidated Table of Cases* to see if there is a reported citation.

Judicial Treatment of Statutes on Rules of Practice (Noting Up a Statute or Rule)

1. When looking up sections of a statute, you should keep in mind that the same section of a statute can be numbered differently over the years. Section 10 in the R.S.O. 1970 statute may be numbered Section 12 in the R.S.O. 1980 version of the statute and another number in the R.S.O. 1990 version of the statute.

   To obtain the history of a section of the statute, you can trace the numbering of the section through the years. At the end of each section in a statute, there is reference to the predecessor section of the section in the previous revised statutes. If there is no reference, the section was passed since the last issue of revised statutes. For example if Section 13 in the R.S.O. 1990 statute refers you to section 12 in the R.S.O. 1980 statute, check the R.S.O. 1980 statute which will in turn refer you to the correct section in the R.S.O. 1970 statute. In this way you can work your way backwards to the act which passed the section you are noting up. You will need these section numbers to note up the section in the *Abridgment*.

NOTE: Since 1988, the *Abridgment* has published an annual volume titled *Canadian Current Law: Legislation Annual*. The legislative history of statutes and regulations from their beginnings in the legislature as bills are traced. The service is kept current with softcover issues of *Canadian Current Law: Legislation*. The disadvantage of the "Legislation" portion of the Abridgment is that it covers such a short time frame. However, if research on a relatively recent statute, with a short legislative history is being performed, the "Legislation" service may be of use to you.

2. Look up the statute, statutory section, or rule in the "Statutes Judicially Considered" permanent volumes of the *Abridgment* (Most recent volumes are titled *Canadian Citations: S.J.C./R.J.C.*). Work through the volumes in chronological order. Be sure to check under the various versions of a statute with the correct section numbers. After the most recent annual volume, check the softcover quarterly supplement. Further update your search by checking the softcover editions of *Canadian Citations: Statutes Judicially Considered*. Your search will be up-to-date as of the date printed on the most recent softcover issue that you consult. To be as current as possible, perform a computer search.

As with the *Canadian Case Citation* portion of the *Abridgment*, symbols are used to indicate what type of consideration has been given to the statute. Symbols in a "circle" denote judicial treatment of a statute or statutory section. Since 1988, the *Abridgment* has indicated the legislative history of statutes by using symbols in "squares".

The symbols appearing in circles that indicate judicial treatment of a statute or statutory section are:

U — Unconstitutional (Where a section of a statute is found to be unconstitutional or invalid by a court)

C — Considered (Where a section of a statute has been considered or analyzed)

R — Referred to (Statute referred to without comment)**this symbol has been discontinued

P — Pursuant to (where a proceeding was undertaken pursuant to a section of a statute)

The symbols appearing in squares that indicate the legislative history of a statute are:

Ad — Added

Am — Amended

Pr — Proclaimed/In force on Assent/Deemed in force

Rp — Repealed

Re — Re-enacted

Rn — Renumbered
Rs — Repealed and new provision substitution

Words and Phrases

1. Check to see if the word or phrase that you are interested in has been considered by checking the *Words & Phrases* volume. If it has been considered, you will find a list of cases under the given word or phrase. This can be further updated by consulting the *Words & Phrases* section in the *General Index* binder and the *Words & Phrases* section in the editions of *Canadian Current Law: Case Law Digests.* Your search will be current as of the date of the last *Current Law* edition that you consulted. To be as current as possible, perform a computer search.

Finding Case Citations

1. Consult the binder of the *Consolidated Table of Cases* that contains case names beginning with the same letter as the case name for which you are searching. You will find your case name listed alphabetically if it has been reported. Under the case name you will find all of the citations for your case. Be sure to check the yellow pages at the beginning of each letter to be absolutely current.

Index to Canadian Legal Literature

1. Consult the discussion on the *Index to Canadian Legal Literature* in this chapter.

CANADIAN LAW ONLINE

In 1992, the publishers of the *Abridgment* introduced *Canadian Law Online* which contains much of the data that is in the *Abridgment* but allows computer access. This book is not concerned with the mechanics of computer searching, however, a knowledge of the features that *Canadian Law Online* shares with the *Canadian Abridgment* is useful:

Case Law Digests:

This feature allows you to find case law by legal issue.

Consolidated Table of Cases:

This feature allows you to search by case name.

Canadian Case Citations:

This feature allows you to "note up" cases.

Canadian Law Online does not charge you for search time. Charges are applied when digests or noting up of cases are requested. The system has been designed so that you can use *Canadian Law Online* to locate the digests you need in the *Abridgment*. Accordingly, you should consider *Canadian Law Online* as an alternative to the *Key and Research Guide* or the *General Index*.

Appendix I

Canadian Abridgment Quick Reference Chart

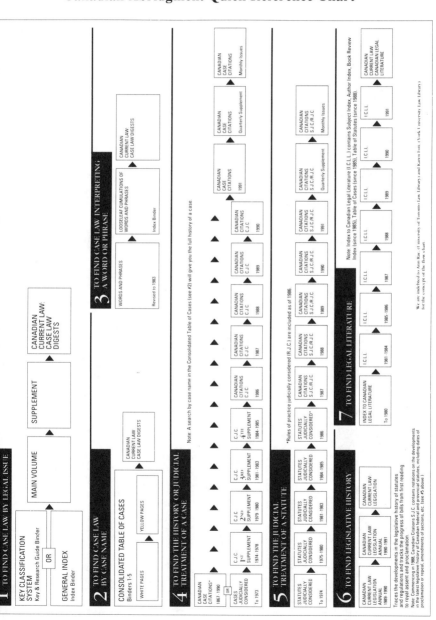

12

Research Tools for Accessing Unreported Decisions

WHAT ARE UNREPORTED DECISIONS?

Unreported decisions are, as their name suggests, decisions that have not been published in a report series. There are two types of unreported decisions:

1.   Decisions that have just been released by a court and may or may not be reported in the future, and
2.   Older decisions that have never been reported.

WHEN ARE UNREPORTED DECISIONS USEFUL?

Usually, the first type of unreported decisions — recent decisions — will be of more use to you. Checking for recent unreported decisions will ensure that your research is absolutely up-to-date.

Having researched your issue using reported sources, you should always update the law you have found by looking for recent unreported decisions. For example, your issue may be answered by a six month old Ontario Court of Appeal case that has been reported. However, you will want to know if there have been any cases since that case that have considered it and whether they have treated the issue in the same manner. You may find that the Court of Appeal of another province has recently followed or declined to follow the case. You may even find that the Ontario Court of Appeal has changed its position on the issue. You may also be interested in examining how the lower courts have responded to the Court of Appeal decision. These more recent decisions will likely be unreported.

Unreported decisions are also useful if you are researching an issue for which you can find nothing in the reported literature, or if you are looking for a case with similar facts to the one you are researching and cannot find one in the reported literature. Just because you cannot find anything on a given issue does not mean that it has not been considered. In these situations, you will be interested in both old and recent unreported decisions.

RESEARCH TOOLS

1.   Legal database systems
     QUIC/LAW

CANLAW
SOQUIJ

2. *All-Canada Weekly Summaries ("A.C.W.S.")*
   A digest, published weekly, of civil cases from across Canada.

3. *Weekly Criminal Bulletin ("W.C.B.")*
   A digest, published weekly, of criminal cases from across Canada.

4. *Alberta Weekly Law Digest ("A.W.L.D.")*
   A weekly digest of Alberta cases dealing with all areas of the law.

5. *British Columbia Weekly Law Digest ("B.C.W.L.D.")*
   A weekly digest of British Columbia cases dealing with all areas of the law.

6. *British Columbia Decisions Criminal Conviction Cases ("B.C.D.C.C.C.")*
   A digest of all British Columbia and Supreme Court of Canada criminal conviction cases, for which the publishers have sufficient information.

7. *British Columbia Decisions Criminal Sentencing Cases ("B.C.D.C.S.C.")*
   A digest of all British Columbia and Supreme Court of Canada criminal sentencing cases, for which the publishers have sufficient information.

8. *Ontario Decisions Criminal Conviction Cases ("O.D.C.C.C.")*
   A digest of all Ontario and Supreme Court of Canada criminal conviction cases, for which the publishers have sufficient information.

9. *Ontario Decisions Criminal Sentencing Cases ("O.D.C.S.C.")*
   A digest of all Ontario and Supreme Court of Canada criminal sentencing cases, for which the publishers have sufficient information.

10. *Supreme Court of Canada Reports Service ("S.C.C.R.S.")*
    A digest of Supreme Court of Canada decisions by year and subject.

11. *Lawyers' Weekly*
    A weekly legal newspaper that discusses recent legal developments

HOW TO USE THE RESEARCH TOOLS

Legal Database Systems

Each Legal Database System has its own organization and its own search strategy. Legal databases are not difficult to use but training is required to give you the ability to formulate the queries so that you will access the information that you seek. We suggest that you obtain such training and learn to use the systems by using them. The ability to do research on the computer is an increasingly important skill.

The main disadvantage to using the computer databases is the expense. Usually charges are based on the amount of time spent by the user. The rates charged depend on the database and the time of day. Students are, however, often given free access to computer databases. We urge you to take advantage of this opportunity to hone your database skills.

A.C.W.S. and *W.C.B.*

A.C.W.S. and *W.C.B.* are softcover booklets that are published on a weekly basis. Eventually, these softcover booklets are replaced by bound volumes. Case digests are organized in alphabetical order by subject in each issue. In order to find cases, turn to the appropriate subject heading and read the cases digested under that heading. If you want a copy of a case, there are instructions about how to order it from the publisher. This of course will involve some expense depending on the number of pages in the case.

To locate case digests in the bound volumes, you can use the Table of Cases and the topical indexes found in each bound volume. You should also check for the index volumes, which are published periodically and consolidate the indexes of several volumes, in order to save time.

A.W.L.D and *B.C.W.L.D*

These digest booklets are published weekly. As with *A.C.W.S.* and *W.C.B.*, the decisions can be ordered from the publisher using the instructions. Bound volumes and cumulative indexes are issued periodically. To locate cases use the topical indexes.

B.C.D.C.C.C., *B.C.D.C.S.C.*, *O.D.C.C.C.*, and *O.D.C.S.C.*

Case digests are published in weekly supplements that are filed in a binder for the current year. The cases are arranged under alphabetically organized subject headings. All years previous to the current year are published in bound volumes and can be accessed through use of the index. Decisions can be ordered according to the instructions given by the publisher.

Lawyers' Weekly

The *Lawyers' Weekly* is a newspaper dealing with issues of interest to Canadian lawyers. Many of its articles deal with recent cases. At the end of each article there are "Full Text" numbers. These are provided so that you can order a copy of the case from the publishers. There is also a section at the back of each issue in which various cases of interest, organized alphabetically by subject area, are digested. Each case digest is accompanied by a Full Text order number. As with the other bulletins, there is a charge involved that is based on the number of pages.

S.C.C.R.S

This digest service for Supreme Court of Canada cases does not provide a means of ordering cases. However, it may be a way to alert you to the existence of a case, which you can then locate quickly on a computer database.

13

Legal Dictionaries (Words and Phrases)

WHAT ARE LEGAL DICTIONARIES?

Legal dictionaries are, as their name suggests, dictionaries that define legal terminology. For the purpose of this book we have a more expansive definition of legal dictionary. We include in the definition of dictionary various tools available for interpreting "words and phrases", since they serve the same conceptual purpose. Words and Phrases dictionaries tell you how the courts define or interpret a word or phrase and provide citations of cases that interpreted the word or phrase.

WHEN DO YOU USE LEGAL DICTIONARIES?

Legal dictionaries are used in two ways:
1. when you need to know the meaning of a legal word or term; or
2. when you need to know how a specific word or phrase has been interpreted judicially.

The difference between these two uses can be demonstrated by examples. An example of a legal term is the word "laches". It refers to the doctrine under which a person can lose his or her legal rights if he or she delays in enforcing them. A source that actually has the label "legal dictionary" should be consulted for this definition.

An example of a word for which you need the interpretation is "highway". There is a layperson's understanding of this word but it has also been the subject of judicial and statutory consideration. A source labelled "legal dictionary" will be useful here, but of even more importance will be the various Words and Phrases tools available.

RESEARCH TOOLS

Canadian Abridgment (the "Abridgment")

The *Abridgment* has a Words and Phrases volume which lists various words and phrases that have been judicially considered and the cases in which they were considered. It is also possible to search for more recent considerations of a given word or phrase using the *Index Binder* and *Current Law: Canadian Case Law Digests*. The disadvantage of the *Abridgment* is that for words and phrases entries prior to September 1992, you have to check each case in order to see how a word or phrase was interpreted, as the *Abridgment* only gives you the case citation. Since September 1992, a quotation from the case has been included.[1]

Sanagan, *The Encyclopedia of Words and Phrases, Legal Maxims, Canada 1825 to 1985*, 4th ed.

This Encyclopedia contains various words and phrases listed alphabetically. Under each word and phrase there are various definitions given along with case citations. When using it, you should also check the updates that are filed at the front of the volumes.

Carswell Topical Report Services

The cumulative indexes, as well as the indexes to each volume of the Carswell Topical Reports Services, contain words and phrases with a listing of cases that have considered the meaning of a given word or phrase.

Yogis, *A Canadian Law Dictionary* 1983

Black's Law Dictionary, 1983

Black's Law Dictionary is an American law dictionary, however, it is used widely in Canadian jurisprudence.

---

1 For more detail on how to use the *Abridgment* Words and Phrases service, see the Words and Phrases section of Chapter Ten.

14

Constitutional Research

WHAT IS CONSTITUTIONAL RESEARCH?

The Constitution is the supreme law of the country and the validity of all other laws is determined by their consistency with the Constitution. Accordingly, an understanding of constitutional research is fundamental to the study or practice of Canadian law.

There are two main categories of constitutional research problems: (a) federalism, and (b) rights and freedoms. When you are given a federalism problem, you will have to determine whether a given law is within the scope of the powers conferred on the federal or provincial governments under the *Constitution Act, 1867*[1] (the "*Constitution Act*"). For instance, the postal service is listed under s. 91 of the *Constitution Act* as a federal power, whereas the regulation of municipalities is listed under s. 92 as a provincial power. Accordingly, the province of Ontario could not pass laws to regulate the postal service, and the federal government could not pass laws to regulate municipalities. Federalism, therefore, deals with the rights between governments.

The second category of constitutional research deals with the rights of individuals and groups as against the state. This category of research involves the *Canadian Charter of Rights and Freedoms*[2] (the "*Charter*"). The *Charter* provides individuals and groups with certain substantive rights and freedoms. The rights and freedoms guaranteed in the *Charter* may, however, be infringed upon by the government if the law or government action is deemed under s. 1 of the *Charter* to be a reasonable limit that is prescribed by law and demonstrably justified in a free and democratic society.

Constitutional research involves two main steps:
1. Determine the meaning of the relevant constitutional provision. This step involves first reading the provision and second finding the case law which has interpreted the provision.
2. Obtain evidence to prove, based on the accepted interpretation of the constitutional provision, that the impugned law or government action is or is not in violation of the Constitution.

---

1 (U.K.), 30 & 31 Vict., c. 3.
2 Part I of the *Constitution Act, 1982*, being Schedule B to the *Canada Act, 1982* (U.K.), 1982, c. 11.

These steps will be described in greater detail below for the two different categories of constitutional problems.

RESEARCHING UNDER THE *CONSTITUTION ACT, 1867*

Interpretation of a Constitutional Provision

To find cases which interpret the provisions of the *Constitution Act*, look up that provision of the Constitution in the *Canadian Citations: Statutes Judicially Considered* portion of the *Canadian Abridgment* (the "*Abridgment*").[3] The Constitution is the first statute you will find listed. Under the relevant provision(s) of the Constitution you will find a list of all of the cases which have considered that provision(s).

As with other types of research, treatises and looseleafs can be useful in assisting you to locate and interpret the leading cases on your topic.[4] However, you should not rely on a treatise or looseleaf to identify all of the case law on your topic. To be thorough, always check the *Canadian Citations: Statutes Judicially Considered* portion of the *Abridgment*.

Historical Element

Research under the *Constitution Act* may have an historical element in two contexts. First, if there is no case law under the provision of the Constitution in which you are researching, you can gain insight into the purpose and intent of the provision by examining the parliamentary debates preceding Confederation. On a number of occasions, the Supreme Court of Canada has looked at the history of a provision of the *Constitution Act* — i.e., what the framers of the Constitution intended for the provision to accomplish — to gain insight into how the provision should be interpreted.[5]

Second, the scope of the rights protected under certain provisions of the *Constitution Act* may be ascertained by an inquiring into the rights in existence at the time of Confederation. For instance, s. 93(1) of the *Constitution Act* provides:

> 93.   In and for each Province the Legislature may exclusively make Laws in relation to Education, subject and according to the following Provisions:
>
> (1)   Nothing in any such Law shall prejudicially affect any Right or Privilege with respect to Denominational Schools which any Class of Persons have by Law in the Province at the Union.

---

3   Consult Chapter Eleven for a discussion of how to use the *Canadian Citations: Statutes Judicially Considered* portion of the *Abridgment*.

4   For a list of looseleaf services and treatises, consult the Constitutional Law section of the Selective Topical Bibliography.

5   For instance, see *Re An Act to Amend the Education Act* [1987] 1 S.C.R. at 1173.

The wording of s. 93(1) makes clear that a province cannot make a law with respect to education which would derogate from a right or privilege enjoyed by denominational schools at the time of Confederation. Thus, to assess whether a provincial law affecting denominational schools is *intra vires*, the rights and privileges of denominational schools at Confederation must be ascertained.[6] This would involve an examination of the legislation affecting denominational schools at the time of Confederation and/or just before.

Another example is s. 96 of the *Constitution Act* which provides:

> 96. The Governor General shall appoint the Judges of the Superior, District, and County Courts in each Province, except those of the Courts of Probate in Nova Scotia and New Brunswick.

The Supreme Court of Canada has set out a three part test to determine whether a power falls within the jurisdiction of a superior, district, or county court:

1. Does the impugned power conform to a power exercised by a superior, district, or county court at Confederation?
2. Is the impugned power "judicial", "administrative", or "legislative"? and
3. Does the power, in its "institutional setting", broadly conform to a s. 96 power?

The first part of the test involves an historical inquiry into the powers of superior, district, or county courts.[7]

When doing historical research under s. 96, you should be aware that prior to Confederation the court structure in Upper Canada conformed to that in England. Accordingly, when inquiring into the powers of the courts at this time, you will not find courts named "superior" or "district" courts. You will, therefore, have to be sensitive to the court structure in England at the time.

In addition, when doing historical research, you should be sensitive to the fact that the terminology used at the time of Confederation might be different than that used today, although the meaning may be the same. For instance, in *Re Residential Tenancies Act, 1979*,[8] the Supreme Court of Canada was asked to determine whether a provincial commission could make orders evicting tenants from residential premises. It was necessary, therefore, to determine whether superior, district or county courts exercised the power of eviction in 1867. At this time, the term "eviction" was not used. Instead, the operative term was "ejectment", which, in fact, means the same thing as eviction. Legal dictionaries often contain historical words

---

6 *Ibid.*, at p. 1177.
7 *Re Residential Tenancies Act*, [1981] 1 S.C.R. 714.
8 *Ibid.*

and phrases and should be consulted to ascertain the meaning of unfamiliar terms.

Government Policy and Social Science Evidence

Evidence such as government reports, law reform commission reports, social science studies, or statistics may be useful in proving or disproving the lawful exercise of legislative authority. These types of sources can provide insight into the social purposes the legislation was intended to achieve, the context against which the legislation was enacted, and the institutional framework in which the legislation is intended to operate. All of these factors may be relevant.

In *Reference re Anti-Inflation Act*,[9] the Supreme Court of Canada was asked to assess whether the federal government's anti-inflation legislation addressed a matter of national importance affecting the peace, order, and good government of Canada. In assessing this question, the court admitted an economic study by Professor Lipsey dealing with the harm caused by inflation, the Canadian inflationary experience, the state of the economy in 1975, and various policy options. Other evidence admitted relating to the then prevailing level of inflation included the White Paper tabled in the House by the Minister of Finance and material from Statistics Canada. Subsequent cases have also relied on evidence of this nature. In *Re Residential Tenancies Act, 1979*, the Supreme Court of Canada indicated that a flexible approach should be adopted with respect to the admissibility of extrinsic materials in government references:

> Material relevant to the issues before the court, and not inherently unreliable or offending against public policy should be admissible, subject to the proviso that such extrinsic materials are not available for the purpose of aiding in statutory construction.[10]

RESEARCHING UNDER THE *CHARTER OF RIGHTS AND FREEDOMS*

Structure of the *Charter*

In order to understand the discussion about researching constitutional issues under the *Charter*, it is necessary to have a basic knowledge of the structure of the *Charter*. While the structure of the *Charter* is much more complex than described below, for the purposes of this discussion on research techniques, we will focus on four main parts of the *Charter*:

---

9 [1976] 2 S.C.R. 373.
10 *Supra*, note 7 at 723.

Part I: Application

Section 32 of the *Charter* indicates that the *Charter* applies to the actions of governments. This means that, for example, your neighbour cannot infringe on your rights and freedoms guaranteed under the *Charter*.

Part II: Substantive Rights and Freedoms

This part of the *Charter* provides substantive rights and freedoms to individuals and groups. The onus is always on the party asserting that a *Charter* violation has occurred to prove such infringement on a balance of probabilities. There are two aspects to consider under this part of the *Charter*:

1. Is the person wishing to mount a *Charter* challenge entitled to do so? (i.e., does the person have standing?)
2. Has a right or freedom under the *Charter* been infringed?

Part III: Governments' Rights to Limit Substantive Rights and Freedoms

Even if your *Charter* rights have been infringed, the government is still given an opportunity under s. 1 to show that such infringement is justified because the government action is a reasonable limit demonstrably justified in a free and democratic society. Under this section, the onus is on the government to prove that the infringement is justified on a balance of probabilities.

Part IV: Remedies Available

If the government did not succeed in establishing that the infringement of the right or freedom under s. 1 is justified, the onus reverts to the plaintiff to prove on the balance of probabilities that he or she is entitled to a particular remedy — i.e., the remedy is necessary to cure the constitutional wrong done to him or her. There are two remedial sections under the *Charter*: s. 24(1) and s. 52(1).

Section 24(1) provides:

> Anyone whose rights or freedoms, as guaranteed by this Charter, have been infringed or denied may apply to a court of competent jurisdiction to obtain such remedy as the court considers appropriate and just in the circumstances.

As the wording of this section indicates, the person must have suffered an infringement of his or her rights or freedoms in order to qualify for a remedy under s. 24(1).

Section 52(1) provides:

The Constitution of Canada is the supreme law of Canada, and any law that is inconsistent with the provisions of the Constitution is, to the extent of the inconsistency, of no force or effect.

Under s. 52(1) declaratory relief is available. This means that the court can declare a law that has been found to be inconsistent with the *Charter*, to be of no force or effect.

Stages of Research

Researching under the *Charter of Rights and Freedoms* (the "Charter") may involves five stages:
1. Does the *Charter* apply?
2. If the answer to the first question is yes, does the party have standing to bring a *Charter* claim?
3. If the answer to the second question is yes, is there an infringement or denial of one of the rights or freedoms guaranteed under the *Charter*?
4. If the answer to the third question is yes, is the denial or infringement justified under s. 1?
5. If the answer to the fourth question is no, what is the appropriate remedy?

Does the Charter apply?

To determine how "government action" has been judicially interpreted, consult looseleaf services on the application of the *Charter* or on s. 32 of the *Charter*. Two particularly useful looseleaf services are: Laskin et al. (eds.), *Canadian Charter of Rights Annotated* (Aurora: Canada Law Book) and Hogg, *Constitutional Law in Canada* 3rd (Toronto: Carswell).[11] If these looseleaf services are not available at your library, consult the *Canadian Case Citations: Statutes Judicially Considered* portion of the *Canadian Abridgment* under s. 32 of the *Charter*.[12] Because new cases are being litigated under the *Charter* daily, you should also always check for recent unreported decisions either by using a computer data base or by using digests such as the *All-Canada Weekly Summaries* and the *Weekly Criminal Bulletin*.[13]

---

11 For a list of other looseleaf services on the *Charter*, consult the Constitutional Law section of the Selective Topical Bibliography.
12 Consult Chapter Eleven for a discussion of how to use the *Canadian Case Citations: Statutes Judicially Considered* portion of the *Abridgment*.
13 For an explanation on how to access unreported decisions, see Chapter Twelve.

Does the Party have Standing to Bring a Charter Claim?

Standing has two aspects, in that you must satisfy the requirements under the section conferring the right or freedom as well as the requirements under one of the remedial sections. You must determine whether or not you have standing at the outset. Obviously, you need recognition under the specific section conferring the right or freedom in order to make a claim. However, it is equally important to research the entitlement to a remedy. If you do not have standing to obtain a remedy, any finding of an infringement may be a hollow victory.

To determine whether you have standing under the substantive right or freedom, refer to the wording of that right or freedom and consult a looseleaf service under the appropriate section of the *Charter*. For example, s. 15 of the *Charter* states:

> Every individual is equal before and under the law and has the right to the equal protection and equal benefit of the law without discrimination and, in particular, without discrimination based on race, national or ethnic origin, colour, religion, sex, age or mental or physical disability.

An individual who has suffered an alleged infringement of his or her rights under s. 15 could bring a claim. However, note that an individual does not include a corporation. Corporations have no standing to raise a s. 15 claim.[14] Corporations do have standing under other sections of the *Charter*. For example, s. 8 of the *Charter*, which protects against unreasonable search and seizure, applies to both individuals and corporations. It is therefore necessary to examine the wording of the *Charter* provision under which you wish to mount your challenge, as well as any applicable case law, in order to see if you satisfy the standing requirement.

To locate jurisprudence on standing — both under the substantive right or freedom and under the remedial sections of the Charter — the same research process we outlined under the above section, "Does the Charter apply?", should be used.

Is there a Charter Infringement?

To assess whether a right or freedom has been infringed or denied, you must determine how the right of freedom in question has been interpreted. For instance, what is the test for assessing whether freedom of expression has been denied under s. 2(*b*)? Or what is the meaning of "arbitrary detention" under s. 9? In the early years of *Charter* jurisprudence, the courts relied on a number of sources when interpreting the open-textured terms of

---

14 *Edmonton Journal v. Alberta (Attorney General)*, [1989] 2 S.C.R. 1326.

the *Charter*, including journal articles by legal scholars,[15] the works of legal theorists and philosophers,[16] and American constitutional jurisprudence.[17] Presently, these sources are being cited less frequently, as there is now a well-developed body of Canadian jurisprudence under most sections of the *Charter*. To locate this jurisprudence, the same research process that we have outlined under the above section, "Does the Charter apply?", should be used.

Once you have ascertained how the right or freedom has been interpreted (i.e. how the right or freedom has been defined and the test for establishing that the right or freedom has been denied), the onus is on the plaintiff to prove on the balance of probabilities that *his or her* right or freedom has been denied. Sometimes it will be possible to prove that a right or freedom has been denied by relying solely on the facts of the case. For instance, to prove that someone has been arbitrarily detained in contravention of s. 9, the manner in which the person was detained would have to be described. These facts must be applied to the Supreme Court of Canada's test for determining: (*a*) what constitutes a detention, and (*b*) what constitutes arbitrariness, for the purpose of s. 9. In this type of a case, it would not be necessary or relevant to introduce government reports, law reform commission reports, or social science evidence to assist in proving the denial of a right or freedom.

In other cases, social science evidence, government reports and other studies may be instrumental in establishing the denial of a right or freedom. For instance, in *R. v. Morgentaler*,[18] the Supreme Court of Canada considered whether s. 251 of the *Criminal Code*,[19] which made abortion an indictable offence unless the majority of members on a "Therapeutic Abortion Committee"[20] determined that the continuation of the pregnancy would

---

15 For instance, in *Law Society of Upper Canada v. Skapinker*, [1984] 1 S.C.R. 357, the Supreme Court of Canada cited with approval an article by John B. Laskin entitled "Mobility Rights under the *Charter*", 4 *Supreme Court L.R.* 89.

16 For instance, in *Retail, Wholesale and Department Store Union v. Dolphin Delivery Ltd.*, [1986] 2 S.C.R. 573 at 583, the Supreme Court of Canada quoted John Stuart Mill on freedom of expression.

17 For instance, in *Hunter v. Southam*, [1984] 2 S.C.R. 145, the Supreme Court of Canada looked at case law decided under the Fourth Amendment of the American *Bill of Rights* to interpret s. 8 of the *Charter*, which guarantees security against unreasonable search and seizure.

18 (1988) 44 D.L.R. (4th) 385 (S.C.C.).

19 R.S.C. 1970, c. C-34.

20 "Therapeutic Abortion Committee" was defined in s. 251 as "a committee comprised of not less than three members each of whom is a qualified medical practitioner, appointed by the board of that hospital for the purpose of considering and determining questions relating to terminations of pregnancy within the hospital".

endanger the woman's life or health, contravenes s. 7 of the *Charter*.[21] In finding that s. 251 deprived women of security of person, the majority of the court relied on a number of studies which documented the delay induced by the requirement of approval by a therapeutic abortion committee[22] and the effect of the delay on the health risks (physical and psychological) associated with such delay.[23] In considering whether this deprivation of security of person was in accordance with principles of fundamental justice, the court also examined a number of reports assessing how s. 251 operated and statistics which addressed whether the procedure for obtaining therapeutic abortions was being applied equitably throughout Canada. Dickson C.J.C. acknowledged:

> As is often the case in matters of interpretation, however, the straightforward reading of this statutory scheme is not fully revealing. In order to understand the true nature and scope of s. 251, it is necessary to investigate the practical operation of the provisions.[24]

An assessment of the "practical operation of legislation" will often entail an examination of government reports, statistics and other studies.

Is the Infringement Justified Under s. 1?

Under s. 1 of the *Charter* the onus is on the government or the defendant to establish on the balance of probabilities that the denial of the right or freedom is "demonstrably justified in a free and democratic society". Your first step is to determine the test for interpreting s. 1. The test was first enunciated by the Supreme Court of Canada in *R. v. Oakes*[25] as follows:

    (*a*) the objective of the impugned law or government action must be of pressing and substantial importance in a free and democratic society;

    (*b*) the measures adopted by the government to obtain its objective must be rationally connected to the objective;

---

21 Section 7 provides "[e]veryone has the right to life, liberty and security of person and the right not to be deprived thereof except in accordance with the principles of fundamental justice."

22 For instance, *The Report of the Committee on the Operation of the Abortion Law* (the "*Badgley Report*") and *The Report on Therapeutic Abortion Services in Ontario* (the "*Powell Report*").

23 For instance, Cates & Grimes, "Deaths from Second Trimester Abortion by Dilation and Evacuation: Causes, Prevention, Facilities" (1981), 58 *Obstetrics and Gynaecology* at 401 & *The Powell Report*.

24 *Supra*, note 16 at 408.

25 [1986] 1 S.C.R. 103.

(c) the law or government action can infringe on the right or freedom no more than is necessary to accomplish the objective ("least drastic means" test); and

(d) the law or government action cannot have a disproportionately severe effect on the persons to whom it applies.

Since the *Oakes* case, subsequent Supreme Court of Canada jurisprudence has modified significantly the test, in particular, the third step of the test: the "least drastic means" requirement.[26] To locate this jurisprudence, the same research process that we have outlined above under the section, "Does the Charter apply?", should be used.

Once you have determined the appropriate test under s. 1, proving that you have met the test will involve tracing the history of the impugned legislation and the use of non-traditional legal research tools.

Tracing the History of the Impugned Legislation

The first requirement of the *Oakes* test is to establish that the purpose of the impugned legislation is of "pressing and substantial" importance in a free and democratic society. To ascertain the purpose, you must trace the history of the legislation to the time in which it was enacted. This historical inquiry is vital because, as Dickson C.J.C. stated in *R. v. Big M Drug Mart*, "Purpose is a function of the intent of those who drafted and enacted the legislation at the time, and not of any shifting variable."[27] Therefore, an objective that did not prompt the enactment of the legislation is irrelevant to the s. 1 inquiry, even if that objective might be considered pressing and substantial today. For instance in *R. v. Zundel*,[28] the history of the impugned legislation was traced back to the thirteenth century. Because the purpose of the legislation at the time of enactment in the thirteenth century is no longer of pressing and substantial importance today, the requirement of the first component of the *Oakes* test was not satisfied. This outcome was dictated by requirements of the *Oakes* test notwithstanding the fact that other arguably pressing and substantial purposes could be ascribed to the legislation today.[29]

Hansard

Federal or provincial *Hansard* can be useful in determining the purpose of the legislation. *Hansard* records everything that is said in the legislature

---

26 See in particular *R. v. Edwards Books & Art Ltd.*, [1986] 2 S.C.R. 713 and *R. v. Irwin Toy Ltd.*, [1989] 1 S.C.R. 927.

27 [1985] 1 S.C.R. 295 at 335.

28 [1992] 2 S.C.R. 731

29 For instructions on how to trace the history of a statutory section, consult Chapter Fifteen.

or House of Commons. To find the appropriate portions of *Hansard*, you will have to trace the history of the legislation to when it was enacted and/or amended.

When reading *Hansard*, you should be aware that all parliamentary debate about the legislation will not be of equal weight or relevance. You should look in particular for the statements of the Minister when she introduced the legislation, as she will generally summarize the objectives of the government in introducing the legislation. Statements by opposition members or backbenchers about the purpose and effects of the legislation will have little or no weight. Legislative debates may also indicate whether alternative legislation or wording was considered, and if so, why it was rejected. Debates which reveal why alternative legislation or wording was rejected may give insight into what the legislators were trying to achieve in enacting the impugned legislation.

Law Reform Commission Reports and Royal Commission Reports

Law Reform Commission Reports[30] and Royal Commission Reports can be useful in assessing the various components of the s. 1 test. These reports often provide in depth analysis of the history of specific legislation, the effects of the legislation on various groups in society and alternative legislation. For instance, in *R. v. Edwards Books & Art Ltd.*[31], a Law Reform Commission Report entitled *Report on Sunday Observance Legislation* (1970) was the only evidence considered for the purpose of s. 1.

Law Reform Commission Reports and Royal Commission Reports are indexed in the *Canadian Abridgment: Index to Canadian Legal Literature.*[32]

Social Science Research

The Supreme Court of Canada has indicated a willingness to admit social science evidence under s. 1 of the Charter. For instance, in the *R. v. Irwin Toy Ltd.,*[33] which involved a challenge to the provisions of the Quebec legislation prohibiting television advertisements directed towards children under 13 years of age, numerous social science studies on the effect of advertising on the development and perceptions of young children were

---

30 See Chapter Eight on Law Reform Commission Reports.

31 [1986] 2 S.C.R. 713.

32 See Chapter Eleven on how to use the *Index to Canadian Legal Literature* portion of the *Abridgment.*

33 (1989), 58 D.L.R. (4th) 577 (S.C.C.).

introduced. In *Ford v. Quebec (A.G.)*[34] case, which involved a challenge to the provisions of the Quebec *Charter of the French Language*[35] requiring that public signs and posters and commercial advertising be in the French language only and that only the French version of a firm name be used, the Attorney General of Quebec introduced studies on sociolinguistics and language planning in addition to articles, reports, and statistics describing the position of the French language in Quebec and Canada that gave rise to and justified the language planning policy reflected in the *Charter of the French Language*.

Social science evidence can be obtained from a wide variety of sources, but an excellent starting place is journal articles. The *Index to Periodical Articles Related to Law* indexes articles which are not strictly legal but have a legal dimension. Non-legal indexes include *PAIS International in Print*, the *Social Sciences Index*, and *Index Medicus*. There are also hundreds of specialized indexing and abstracting services.

Legislation from Other Jurisdictions

With respect to item three of the *Oakes* test (minimal impairment test), as modified by subsequent case law, it can be useful to compare the impugned legislation with legislation in other jurisdictions (in Canada and abroad). Inquire whether other jurisdictions have legislation which seeks to achieve the same objective as the impugned legislation. If so, does this legislation achieve its objective in a manner that results in a less serious denial of a right or freedom than the impugned legislation, or is the impugned legislation comparable with the legislation in other jurisdictions.

For instance, in the *Irwin Toy* case,[36] the Supreme Court in assessing whether Quebec legislation imposing a ban on commercial advertising directed at children was justified under s. 1, concluded that the ban was not out of proportion to measures taken in other jurisdictions. In particular, the Court took note of similar legislation in Belgium, Denmark, Norway, and Sweden, and of the fact that throughout Canada, the public network does not accept children's commercials (with the exception of the CBC during "family programmes").

Often comparative legislation will be examined in Law Reform Commission Reports, Royal Commission Reports, journal articles, and other studies. The researcher will save time by checking such sources first.

---

34 (1988), 54 D.L.R. (4th) 577 (S.C.C.).
35 R.S.Q. 1977, c. C-11, ss. 58 and 69.
36 *Supra*, footnote 32.

What is the Appropriate Remedy?

The researcher should examine what other types of remedies have been granted in similar cases and determine the legal tests which must be met to obtain particular remedies. This can be done by locating the jurisprudence under s. 24(1) or s. 52(1) of the *Charter* in a looseleaf service. To locate this jurisprudence, the same research process that we have outlined under the above section, "Does the Charter apply?", should be used.

15

Researching Statutes

WHAT ARE STATUTES?

Statutes or Acts are a source of law. They are enacted by governments to codify the common law, reform the common law and/or deal with issues not addressed by the common law.

Statutes are written according to a standard format. Each statute is assigned a chapter designation which you will need to know for citation purposes. The "long title", as its name suggests, is a lengthy and detailed title for the statute. Long titles usually begin with the phrase "An Act respecting . . ." They are useful because they provide a description of the subject matter of the statute and can be cited in court as an interpretive aid. Statutes also usually have short titles. These are typically preceded by the phrase "This Act may be cited as . . ." The actual text of the statute is written with numbered and alphabetized section and paragraph numbers for easy citation.

Usually at or near the beginning of the statute, you will find a definition section which defines terminology that is used in the statute. Application sections, which indicate the situations to which the statute is expected to apply, are also common. Brief notes usually appear in the margin of the statute that indicate the subject matter of various sections. For example, the word "Limitation" in a margin note indicates that the section contains a limitation period. Margin notes are useful tools for finding your way around a statute, but they do not constitute part of the statute, as passed by the legislature, and therefore cannot be used for interpretive purposes.

HOW ARE STATUTES MADE AND AMENDED?

Statutes are created and amended by bills. Federal bills may originate from either the chamber of Parliament, the House of Commons or the Senate. Provincial bills originate in the provincial legislature.

In order for a federal bill to become law, the bill must be read and voted on three times by both the House of Commons and the Senate. Provincial bills must be read and voted on three times by the legislature. The statute comes into force when it receives Royal Assent and is proclaimed or both.

On "first reading", the bill is introduced and copies of it are distributed. On "second reading", the bill is fully debated by the Legislative House and referred to a committee which will study the bill and propose amendments.

On "third reading", the amendments are considered by the House and the bill is voted on. At the federal level, the bill will then go through the same process in the Senate or the House, depending on where the bill originated.

WHEN IS A STATUTE "IN FORCE"?

A statute may:

(*a*) specify the actual date on which the statute will come into force;

(*b*) state that the statute will come into force upon receiving *Royal Assent*; or

(*c*) state that the statute will come into force on a date fixed by *Proclamation*.

The date on which *Royal Assent* was given is shown on the sessional volume of the statute right after the title of the statute.

Proclamation dates can be found in the latest sessional volume under the heading "Proclamations". Each issue of *Canadian Current Law* ("*Current Law*") also contains a heading entitled "Statutes Amended, Repealed, or Proclaimed in Force".

Sometimes statutes do not specify when they come into force. In these instances, you should check the relevant interpretation act in your jurisdiction to ascertain when the statute would come into force. For example, federal, Nova Scotia, and British Columbia statutes making no such specification come into force upon receiving Royal Assent.[1] Ontario statutes making no such specification come into force on the later of: (*a*) 60 days after the prorogation of the session in which the Act was passed, or (*b*) 60 days after signification.[2]

HOW ARE STATUTES PUBLISHED?

Sessional or Annual Volumes

Sessional volumes contain statutes (and amendments thereto) passed during a session of Parliament or legislature. Annual volumes contain statutes (and amendments thereto) passed in a given year. The provisions of a statute that have been amended many times will likely be spread over a number of annual volumes. Within any volume or set of volumes the organizing scheme is alphabetic.

At the federal level, prior to 1984, all statutes passed during a session of Parliament were bound in sessional volumes. Sessions can cover more

---

1 *Interpretation Act*, R.S.C. 1985 c. I-21, s. 5(1); *An Act Respecting the Form and Interpretation of Statutes*, R.S.N.S. 1989, c. 235, s. 3(2); and *Interpretation Act*, R.S.B.C. 1979, c. 206, s. 3(1).

2 *Statutes Act*, R.S.O. 1990, c. S.21, s. 5(1).

than one year. As of 1984, federal statutes were published in annual volumes.

Revised Statutes

Every ten or fifteen years, statutes published in the sessional or annual volumes are consolidated into a bound master set of statutes.[3] The revised statute replaces and consolidates most of the sessional volumes or annual volumes preceding it as the official text of the statute. However, note that some obscure statutes may not be included in the consolidation.

An alternative to the bound volume format for publication of statutes is the looseleaf format. Some provinces, such as British Columbia and Nova Scotia, have abandoned the bound format altogether and only publish their statutes in the looseleaf format.

Looseleafs are published in binders so that new amendments or other developments can be inserted on a regular basis. You should be aware that many looseleaf services are published by commercial publishers. These commercial services, while very useful for research purposes, do not have legal effect and should not be cited. When citing a statute, always cite the official version which is published by the government printers.

In the revised version, whether in bound or looseleaf format, statutes are ordered alphabetically and given consecutive chapter numbers.

Statute Citators

Statute Citators ("Citators") are looseleaf services which show the current state of the statutes since the publication of the latest revised statutes. Cases interpreting sections of the statute are also digested.
NOTE: Tax statutes are not covered in the citators. There are many commercial services that deal exclusively with tax statutes.[4]

DOING STATUTORY RESEARCH

Statutory research involves four steps:
1. determining whether a *relevant statute exists*;
2. *locating* the statute;
3. *updating* the statute; and
4. checking whether the sections of the statute you are concerned with have been *judicially considered.*

---

3 For instance, the latest consolidation of federal statutes occurred as of 1985.
4 See the Tax section in the Selective Topical Bibliography.

Step One: How to Determine Whether a Statute Exists

Texts and Encyclopedias

You should begin your research by looking for your topic in a treatise, the *Canadian Encyclopedic Digest*, or a looseleaf service. These sources may refer you to the name and citation of the relevant statute, if one exists.

Table of Public Statutes

The "Table of Public Statutes" in the latest sessional volume provides an alphabetical listing of those statutes included in the last consolidation and any new statutes that have been passed since the last consolidation. You can skim the list to determine if there are any statutes on your topic. The titles of statutes are generally suggestive of their subject. However, we do not recommend relying on the Table of Public Statutes alone. Sometimes, there may be a subject index that lists relevant statutes by subject. Unfortunately, these do not always exist.

Step Two: How to Locate Statutes

Looseleafs and Office Consolidations

Always begin by checking if there is:
(*a*) a looseleaf version of the statute; or
(*b*) an office consolidation.
If both a looseleaf and office consolidation exist, we recommend using the looseleaf.

Looseleaf services are published in binders so that new developments in the law can be inserted regularly and obsolete law removed. These services save having to update the statute by referring to the sessional or annual volumes and the Citator. The text of the statute will be up-to-date, at minimum, as of the date in which the looseleaf was last updated. The front page of the looseleaf service usually indicates when the looseleaf was last updated.[5]

As noted above, there may be commercial and official looseleaf services. Commercial services do not have legal effect and should not be cited. When citing a statute, always cite the official version which is published by the government printers.

Office consolidations are published by the government. Unlike looseleaf services, office consolidations are not published in binders and, there-

---

5 A more detailed discussion of looseleaf services is found at Chapter Nine. Refer also to the Selective Topical Bibliography for a selective list by subject of looseleaf services.

fore, cannot be updated on a regular basis. Using an office consolidation may still involve referring to some of the sessional volumes and the Citator, depending on the date of the consolidation.

NOTE: Looseleafs or office consolidations are rarely absolutely current. Some of the latter steps enumerated below for updating statutes may have to be followed, even when using a looseleaf or office consolidation.

Step Three: Updating Your Statutes

We outline how to update federal, British Columbia, Nova Scotia, and Ontario statutes. If you need to do research on statutes from provinces, other than the ones with which we deal in this book, the general principles given here should be helpful.[6] The basic method of finding and updating statutes in the various provinces and territories is similar. Depending on the services to which your law library subscribes, the steps may differ slightly from those outlined here but the basic approach is the same.

Federal Statutes

1. Locate your statute in the *Canada Statute Citator* (the "*Citator*"). The Statute is up-to-date as of the date on the lower right-hand side of the page.
2. Check the green pages of the *Citator* ("Monthly Bulletin") to see if there have been any more recent amendments to the statute. If the statute you are researching is not listed, there have been no amendments. The statute is now up-to-date as of the date indicated on the top of page one of the latest Bulletin.
3. Check the individual parts of the *Canada Gazette, Part III* that were published subsequent to the latest Bulletin in the *Citator*. ALTERNATIVELY, check the issues of *Canadian Current Law: Legislation*, subsequent to the date of the latest Bulletin, under the name of your statute in the "Progress of Bills" section of *Canadian Current Law: Legislation*.
4. Telephone the House of Commons and ask for a Procedural Clerk (922-2038) to be up-to-the minute accurate.

British Columbia Statutes

The *Revised Statutes of British Columbia* are published in looseleaf form that is easy to update.

---

6 See also Mary Jane T. Sinclair, *Updating Statutes and Regulations for All Canadian Jurisdictions* 3rd (Ottawa: Canadian Law Information Council, 1989).

1. Your statute is current as of the date on the top of the "User's Guide", found at the beginning of each volume. Disregard the dates printed on the pages of the actual statute, for the purpose of currency.

2. Check the "Status Sheet" at the beginning of each statute for greater detail about the status of the statute — whether portions of the statute are in force, amendments not yet in force, or if the particular statute has been updated beyond the date given on the "User's Guide" at the beginning of the volume.

3. For amendments subsequent to the *Revised Statutes of British Columbia*, locate your statute in the *British Columbia Statute Citator* (the "Citator"). The *Citator* is up-to-date as of the date on the release sheet filed at the front of the volume.

4. Check the title index in the *British Columbia Legislative Digest* for the title of your statute. This digest will tell you the title of Bills introduced and Acts affected. It is updated on a weekly basis. To ascertain the exact nature of the amendment, you will have to refer to a copy of the Bill and read the amending legislation.
    ALTERNATIVELY, refer to the "Progress of Bills" section in editions of *Canadian Current Law: Legislation* subsequent to the release date in the *Citator*, under the name of your statute.

5. Telephone the Office of the Clerk at (604) 387-3785 for the most up-to-date information on the status of your Bill.

Nova Scotia Statutes

The *Revised Statutes of Nova Scotia* are published in a convenient looseleaf form that is easy to update.

1. Your statute is current as of the date on the top of the "User's Guide", found at the beginning of each volume. For the purpose of currency, disregard the dates printed on the pages of the actual statute.

2. For amendments subsequent to the *Revised Statutes of Nova Scotia*, locate your statute in the *Nova Scotia Statute Citator* (the "Citator"). The *Citator* is up-to-date as of the date on the release sheet filed at the front of the volume.

3. Refer to the "Progress of Bills" section in editions of *Canadian Current Law: Legislation* subsequent to the release date in the *Citator*, under the name of your statute.

4. Phone the Nova Scotia Government Bookstore at (902) 424-7580 for the most up-to-date information on the status of your Bill.

Ontario Statutes

1. Locate your statute in the *Ontario Statute Citator* (the *"Citator"*). Amendments subsequent to the Revised Statutes of Ontario 1990 are listed here. The Statute is up-to-date as of the date on the lower right hand side of the page.

2. Check the pink pages of the *Citator* ("Monthly Bulletin"), which are filed in the front section of Binder One, to see if there have been any more recent amendments to the statute. If the statute you are researching is not listed, there have been no amendments. The statute is now up-to-date as of the date indicated on the top of page 1 of the latest Bulletin.

   ALTERNATIVELY, if you do not have access to the *Citator*, you can update the statute by reference to the Table of Public Statutes in the latest annual volume. This table will list all of the amendments made to a given statute since the last revised version of the statute was printed or since the statute was passed, if it was passed in a year subsequent to the issue of the last revised statutes. To update the text of the statute, you will have to look up all of the references to the *Ontario Gazette* listed there. This is a more time consuming method then using the *Citator*.

3. Check the "Progress of Bills" sections of *Canadian Current Law: Legislation* in issues subsequent to the release date on the *Citator* under the name of your statute.

4. Telephone the Clerk of the House (325-7350) or Legislative Counsel (326-2841) for the most up-to-date information on the status of your Bill.

Step Four: Statutory Interpretation

Judicial Consideration

Cases wherein the courts have interpreted the provisions of a statute are highly relevant.[7] Accordingly, you should always check for judicial consideration of the provisions of the statute you are researching. This jurisprudence may be found in:

(a) the *Statute Citator* (but only since the revision was published — for example, federally since 1985 and in Ontario since 1990); and

---

7 In contrast, if there is case law that predates the statute that is in conflict with the statute, the statute will take precedence.

(*b*) the Canadian Case Citations: Statutes Judicially Considered section of the *Canadian Abridgment*.[8]

You should also always trace the history of the statute — for example, how the section numbers have changed since the original enactment of the section.

Tracing the History of a Statute or Statutory Section

An understanding of the history of the statutory provision you are researching, and how it has changed over time, may help you to interpret the provision.

To obtain the history of a statute or section thereof, trace the versions of the statute or section as they have been published over the years. At the end of each section in a statute, there is a reference to a predecessor section in the previous revised statutes. If there is no reference, the section was passed since the last issue of revised statutes. For example, if s. 13 in the R.S.O. 1990 statute refers you to s. 12 in the R.S.O. 1980 statute, check the R.S.O. 1980 statute which will, in turn, refer you to the correct section in the R.S.O. 1970 statute. In this way, you can work your way backwards to the Act which passed the section you are tracing. Certain statutes are very old and you may find that you can trace the statute back to an English predecessor. You must continue tracing the history of the statute backwards through the English statutes in order to have absolutely complete research. Depending on the scope of your research task, this may not always be necessary or appropriate.

Since 1988, the *Canadian Abridgment* has included a service called *Canadian Current Law: Legislation* which has annual volumes and regular supplements. This service, since 1988, indicates the history of statutes and legislation. If you are dealing with legislation that you know was enacted during or since 1988, you can use this service.

Interpretation Acts

Most jurisdictions have an interpretation act which defines rules and principles of statutory interpretation and construction. Always check the "application" section of the act, which is normally at or near the beginning of the statute, to see if the use of the interpretation act is appropriate. Generally, the principles set out in an interpretation act will apply unless they are inconsistent with the objectives or provisions of the statute subject to interpretation.

---

8 See Chapter Eleven on how to use the *Canadian Case Citations: Statutes Judicially Considered* portion of the *Canadian Abridgment*.

Rules of Statutory Interpretation

There are certain maxims or golden rules of statutory interpretation on which courts rely when the wording of a statute is ambiguous. These rules can be found in treatises on statutory interpretation.[9] The *Canadian Encyclopedic Digest* also has a chapter on statutory interpretation.

Words and Phrases

When the provision of the statute that you are researching has not been judicially considered, there may be a word or phrase in the provision which has been interpreted in other contexts. In these circumstances, it is useful to consult one or more of the Words and Phrases tools.[10]

Hansard

Hansard is the record of everything said in the House of Commons or the provincial legislatures. There is a separate Hansard for each provincial legislature and for the House of Commons. Before legislation is passed, the meaning, purpose, and potential impact of the legislation is debated in the legislature. Courts have indicated some willingness to consider Hansard as an aid for interpreting the intent of legislation where the wording is vague.[11]

When reading *Hansard*, you should be aware that all parliamentary debate about the legislation will not be of equal weight or relevance. Look, in particular, for the statements of the Minister when he or she introduced the legislation, as he will generally summarize the objectives of the government in introducing the legislation. Statements by opposition members or backbenchers about the purpose and effects of the legislation will have little or no weight. Legislative debates may also indicate whether alternative legislation or wording was considered, and if so, why it was rejected. Debates which reveal why alternative legislation or wording was rejected may give insight into what the legislators were trying to achieve in enacting the impugned legislation.

---

9 See Selective Topical Bibliography for a selective list of treatises on statutory interpretation.

10 See Chapter Thirteen on how to use these tools.

11 For instance, see *Reference re Authority of Parliament in Relation to Upper House*, [1980] 1 S.C.R. 54 at 66.

16

Researching Regulations

WHAT ARE REGULATIONS?

Regulations are rules made pursuant to a statute and are known as subordinate legislation. Regulations typically provide necessary detail to broad statutory provisions and enumerate how the provisions of a statute are to be implemented.

HOW ARE REGULATIONS PUBLISHED?

Regulations are published in the *Canada Gazette* and in the various provincial gazettes. Like statutes, regulations are consolidated periodically. For instance, federal regulations were last consolidated in 1978 in the *Consolidated Regulations of Canada*, 1978 ("*C.R.C.*"). The text of the regulations published after the bound consolidated volumes are found in the *Canada Gazette*.

WHEN IS A REGULATION IN FORCE?

Unless stated otherwise in the regulation, federal regulations come into force on the day they are registered. If a regulation is exempt from registration, it comes into force on the day on which it was made or on a date specified in the regulations.[1]

To determine when a provincial regulation comes into force, you should check the Regulation Act of your province or territory. The regulations for British Columbia, Nova Scotia and Ontario come into force on the day they are filed or registered, unless otherwise specified in the regulation. The registration or filing date of a regulation can usually be found just before the text of the regulation or under the title of the regulation. In order for a regulation to come into force before the regulation is filed, the Act under which the regulation was made must authorize it to come into force on an earlier date.[2]

---

1 *Statutory Instruments Act*, R.S.C. 1985, c. S-22, s. 9.
2 *Regulations Act*, S.B.C. 1983, c. 10, s. 4; *An Act to Provide for the Central Filing, Publication and Consolidation of Regulations*, R.S.N.S. 1989, c. 393, s. 3(6); and *Regulations Act*, R.S.O. 1990, c. R.21, s. 3.

DOING REGULATORY RESEARCH

Regulatory research involves three steps:
1. determining whether a *relevant regulation exists* and *locating* it;
2. *updating* the regulation;
3. *interpreting* the regulation.

Step One: How to Determine whether a Regulation Exists and Locate it

Looseleaf Version of Statutes and Regulations

Always begin by checking to see if a *looseleaf* version of the statute and regulation exists. Looseleaf services are published in binders so that changes in the regulations can be inserted regularly and obsolete regulations removed. Beware, however, that looseleafs are only current as of the date on which they were last updated (usually indicated at the front of the looseleaf).[3]

Using the Statutes, Orders and Regulations Portion of the Gazette

If you know the name of the enabling statute under which the regulations you are interested in were enacted, consult the "Table of Regulations by Statute" in the *Statutes, Orders and Regulations* portion of the *Gazette* for the jurisdiction in which you are doing research. You will find an alphabetical listing of all statutes. In turn, under each statute, you will find a listing of the regulations made pursuant to that statute and their citations.

If you know the name of the regulation(s), but not the name of the enabling *statute*, consult the alphabetical listing of regulations in the *Statutes Orders and Regulations* portion of the *Gazette* for the region in which you are doing research. You will be referred to the name of the enabling statute. You must now refer to the "Table of Regulations by Statute" for the citation of the regulation(s).

Step Two: How to Update Regulations

We outline below how to update federal, British Columbia, Nova Scotia, and Ontario regulations. The basic method of finding and updating regulations in the various provinces and territories is similar. If you need to do research on regulations from provinces, other than the ones with which we deal in this book, the instructions given here should be helpful.[4]

---

3 See Chapter Nine on how to use and update looseleaf services.
4 See also Mary Jane T. Sinclair, Updating Statutes and Regulations for All Canadian Jurisdictions (3rd) (Ottawa: Canadian Law Information Council, 1989).

Federal Regulations

1. Update the *Canada Gazette, Part II Statutes, Orders and Regulations* by consulting the bi-weekly issues of the *Canada Gazette Part II*.
    ALTERNATIVELY, you can consult the "Regulations" section in *Canadian Current Law: Legislation*.
                             OR
2. Consult the most recent edition of Carswell's *Canada Regulation Index*. This service lists all federal statutes alphabetically. Below each statute you will find listed the names and citations of the regulations prescribed under that statute. You are current as of the date at the bottom of the first page of the Index.
3. Update by consulting the blue pages at the front of Binder I of the *Canada Regulation Index*. The blue pages are a cumulative update of regulations published on a monthly basis.
4. Update by consulting the bi-weekly editions of the *Canada Gazette* which were published after the date at the bottom of the first page of the most recent edition of the *Canada Regulation Index*.
    ALTERNATIVELY, you can consult the "Regulations" section in *Canadian Current Law: Legislation*.

British Columbia Regulations

1. Consult the Table of Contents in the looseleaf volumes entitled *Consolidated Regulations of British Columbia*. Regulations that are in force can be found under the titles of their respective enabling statutes which are organized alphabetically.
    ALTERNATIVELY, you can consult the listing of regulations currently in force in the *British Columbia Statute Citator* (the "*Citator*"). In the *Citator*, regulations are found under the titles of their enabling statutes.
2. Update the *Consolidated Regulations of British Columbia* by looking through the relevant issues of the *British Columbia Gazette Part II*.
    ALTERNATIVELY, you can consult the "Regulations" section in *Canadian Current Law: Legislation*.

Nova Scotia Regulations

Nova Scotia regulations are poorly organized. There is no consolidated version.

1. Consult the latest annual index of the *Nova Scotia Royal Gazette Part II* under the name of the enabling statute. This will tell you

any regulations passed under that enabling statute for the year of the annual index that you are consulting.

2. If you are unsuccessful in finding the regulation that you are seeking in the latest annual index, you will have to repeat the process of consulting annual indexes going back through the years to 1977.

3. If you did not find the regulation in step two, for the period of time between 1977 and 1973, consult the *Tabled Regulations of Nova Scotia* that were published sessionally.

4. If you did not find the regulation in step three, consult the index in *Statutes of Nova Scotia 1970-1971*, which covers the regulations published in the 1942 consolidation of regulations and those contained in the sessional volumes published between 1942 and 1970.

5. Assuming that you have found nothing in all of the above steps, the regulation you are looking for may be a very recent regulation. You can find very recent regulations in the current issues of the *Nova Scotia Royal Gazette Part II* and the "Regulations" section in *Canadian Current Law: Legislation*.

Ontario Regulations

1. Consult the most recent edition of *Carswell's Regulation Service*. This service lists all Ontario statutes alphabetically. Below each statute you will find listed the names and citations of the regulations prescribed under that statute. You are current as of the date at the bottom of the first page of the Index.

2. Locate more recent regulations by consulting the yellow supplementary pages of *Carswell's Regulation Service*. This will provide you with a listing of regulations current as of the date on the first yellow page.

3. Update by checking those issues of the *Ontario Gazette* which have been published since the date on the first yellow page of *Carswell's Regulation Service*.
    ALTERNATIVELY, you can consult the "Regulations" section in *Canadian Current Law: Legislation*.

OR

1. Consult the *Ontario Regulation Service* which is a looseleaf index that lists all regulations under Ontario statutes. Statutes are listed alphabetically and the names and citations of the regulations are listed under the relevant statute.

2. Update by checking those issues of the *Ontario Gazette* which have been published since the latest edition of the *Ontario Regulation Service*.

ALTERNATIVELY, you can consult the "Regulations" section in *Canadian Current Law: Legislation*.

Step Three: Interpreting Regulations

Regulations are not typically the subject of judicial consideration. To obtain guidance on the interpretation and administration of regulations, you should contact the appropriate government ministry. Sometimes there are policy manuals or guidelines on the administration of regulations which you may be able to obtain.[5]

---

5 For further details, see Chapter Seventeen.

17

Other Legal Research Tools

The purpose of this chapter is to encourage the use of less obvious research tools, some of which are not found in the law library. Effective legal research can encompass the use of resources beyond the library.

GOVERNMENT TELEPHONE DIRECTORIES

It is doubtful that you can complete your research by making one phone call. Indeed, you should always verify any information that you are told. However, a phone call to a knowledgeable person can reduce your research time dramatically by pinpointing exactly where you should look in the library. There are even some research problems for which there is no answer in the library because they fall within the purview of administrative practice rather than law. For such problems, a letter or phone call to the responsible government body is the only way of obtaining the information that you need.

Remember that the government legal services branches act as counsel to the government and are not permitted to provide legal advice to the public. However, some government lawyers may be willing to discuss a legal problem in general terms. If you want to know how a specific statute(s) or regulation(s) is interpreted or administered, you should contact the responsible branch, board, or agency. Statutes and regulations often use intentionally vague and ambiguous language. In addition, many statutes, sections thereof, and regulations have not been judicially considered. Nevertheless, the government body which administers the legislation may have its own interpretation. Often policy guidelines or manuals, containing the Ministry's interpretation of legislation and setting out how the legislation is to be administered, exist. Even when there are no written guidelines, the government body will often have informal guidelines or practices. Knowledge of these guidelines or practices can be vital to satisfying your clients' needs.

When you make a phone call always obtain the names of the people to whom you speak and their official titles. Also keep a record of the date and time of your conversation and the number that you called. Often you will have to try a series of telephone numbers before you find the person who you need. In the event that you need to call back for additional information, you will have an organized record of your previous conversation. This information is also useful to include in a reporting memorandum.

The federal and provincial governments publish government telephone directories. These directories are organized, first by ministry, and then further subdivided by ministerial department. The title and telephone number for each civil servant is listed. As government telephone directories are very detailed, it is more time efficient to use them than a regular telephone book that will only give you the general information number for the relevant ministry.

DATABASES OF MEMORANDA OF LAW

If you are employed by a law firm, the legal department of a government ministry or company, or by a legal aid clinic, there may be an organized repository of past research memoranda that have been completed on various issues to satisfy the research demands of previous files. You may find a memorandum on exactly the same issue or on a related issue. Naturally, you should verify and update any information you find there.

The Ontario Legal Aid Plan has a memoranda database. There is no charge for these memoranda for Ontario Legal Aid cases. All others wanting to use the database may obtain copies of memoranda for a fee. The focus of the database is Criminal law and procedure and Family law. There are a limited number of memoranda on various civil law topics.

LEGAL PUBLISHERS' MAILING LISTS

An inexpensive way to increase your awareness of the ever multiplying legal resources available is to contact the major Canadian legal publishers, request their catalogues, and have your name placed on their mailing lists. When you have a research problem you can scan their catalogues quickly to see if there are any materials published that would help you. If you are on their mailing lists, you will also receive notices of the publication of new materials as they become available. The major Canadian legal publishers are:

Butterworths
Canada Law Book
Carswell/Thompson
CCH (Commerce Clearing House)
Emond Montgomery

SOCIAL SCIENCE RESEARCH

Social science literature may be very useful in building a case, particularly when the law in the area has not been clearly defined or requires reform. Law does not operate in a vacuum. It is part of the social fabric and must change to reflect changes in society and to achieve the ultimate goal of justice. The social sciences of economics, psychology, sociology, and criminology are used and referred to frequently by courts.

A recent illustration of this practice is the Supreme Court of Canada's decision in *R. v. Lavallee*.[1] Prior to this decision, it was virtually impossible for battered women who killed their abusive spouses to make a case of self-defense. In order to prove the classic elements of a defense of self-defense, there must be an imminent threat of death or grave bodily harm. However, battered women who kill their abusive spouses in self-defense will generally do so when the harm is not imminent in the traditional sense. The Supreme Court of Canada's decision in *Lavallee* expanded the defense of self-defense by drawing on the psychological literature on battered women's syndrome. This decision shows the vital role social science literature can play in developing the law.

Social science evidence is often frequently referred to in *Charter* cases. Such evidence can be useful both in proving that a right or freedom has been infringed and in proving that the infringement is justified under section 1.[2]

To access social science literature an excellent resource is the *Index to Periodicals Related to Law*. This index covers articles published throughout the English-speaking world on social science and scientific, and medical topics that have legal dimensions.[3] Non-legal indexes include *PAIS International in Print*, the *Social Sciences Index*, and *Index Medicus*. There are also hundreds of specialized indexing and abstracting services.

SPECIALIZED INDUSTRIAL PERIODICALS

If a client is involved in a certain industry, it may be necessary for their lawyers to understand the industry in order to negotiate or litigate effectively. If this sort of information is required check to see if there is a specialized trade journal. There are thousands of trade journals. Do not let the apparent obscurity of the client's business stop you from looking.

PRESS REPORTS

There are a large number of computer databases that carry the full text of various news publications. It is not uncommon for large law firms to make regular use of these. Accessing these databases requires trained search skills and money. Usually librarians will perform your searches for you. As

---

1 [1990] 1 S.C.R. 852.

2 For a discussion of the use of social science evidence under the *Charter of Rights and Freedoms*, see Chapter Fourteen.

3 Consult Chapter Six for a discussion of how to use periodical indexes.

a researcher, you should recognize what type of information is available and how it can be useful.

Reports on On-Going Litigation

You may wish to monitor a case that is of interest to an area of law or a client.

Reports on how Other Cases have Settled

If your client is involved in litigation, this information can help in the negotiation process.

Reports on Similar Fact Situations

You may find that there are no similar fact accident cases but that similar accidents have occurred and have been resolved out of court. Such information can be valuable in settlement negotiations or litigation.

Background on Clients or Potential Clients, Other Parties, Lawyers, and Judges

This type of information obviously has as many uses as the type of information available. For example, you may discover that a potential client has engaged and fired three law firms in the last year. This may influence a decision about whether the firm should seek this party's business.

MARTINDALE-HUBBELL LAW DIRECTORY

Martindale-Hubbell is an American publication that has a number of useful features.

Profiles

Martindale-Hubbell lists and profiles lawyers and law firms in the United States and Canada, as well as many countries throughout the world. Its listings for the United States and Canada are particularly comprehensive.

International Law Digest Volume

This volume contains very pithy summaries of the law in all of the countries covered by *Martindale-Hubbell*. They are written by respected practitioners in the various countries. Obviously, consulting *Martindale-Hubbell* does not constitute more than a very brief glimpse of the law in foreign jurisdictions. However, this quick look, combined with a list of qualified practitioners in the relevant jurisdiction, can be very useful when helping a client with foreign interests.

Listing of all Judges in U.S. Federal Court System and Text of the Uniform Acts and A.B.A. Codes

The value of these features is discussed in the chapter on American research.

18

English Legal Research

INTRODUCTION

This chapter is not a comprehensive examination of English legal research, however, it does outline how to use the basic English legal research tools. When doing Canadian legal research, it is often necessary to examine English legal resources. This chapter is written for those doing research on a Canadian legal problem who need to look at English legal materials.

English law is important to Canadian legal research because it forms the basis of our own law. The law of each province is based on the English statute and case law that existed at the time that the province joined Confederation. Until 1949, the Judicial Committee of the Privy Council was the final court of appeal from the Supreme Court of Canada. Accordingly, many older English cases are law in Canada, while more recent developments in English jurisprudence are influential, particularly when there is no Canadian law on the topic or the Canadian law is in a state of confusion. Well respected English texts are also cited with approval in Canadian courts.

APPROACHING ENGLISH LEGAL RESEARCH

Our basic approach to English Legal research is the same as our approach to Canadian legal research. You should commence your research by consulting secondary sources like legal encyclopedias, treatises, periodicals, and looseleafs. These sources should outline the basic principles of the area of the law that you are researching and direct you to the leading cases and relevant statutes. You should then consult any topical law reports or digests that are available. Finally, you should update the case and statutory law on which you wish to rely.

THE ENGLISH COURT STRUCTURE

The English court structure, like Canada's court structure, is hierarchical. It is important to have an understanding of the court structure, since higher court decisions are most persuasive.

The English court structure has been altered periodically, but it is currently organized as follows:

1. County, local and special courts (e.g. Industrial Relations Court)
2. Criminal Court, and the three divisions of the High Court of Justice: Queen's Bench Division, Chancery Division, and Family Division
3. Court of Appeal
4. House of Lords

There is no rule against the citation of low level courts' decisions, but you should, where possible, try to cite Court of Appeal or House of Lords' decisions, which are more persuasive.

LEGAL ENCYCLOPEDIA

Halsbury's Laws of England (3rd Edition)

Halsbury's is an encyclopedia of English law in a set of volumes, in which the law is organized alphabetically by subject. Relevant cases and statutes appear in footnotes. In order to access the relevant volume, you can use the *General Index* which will in turn refer you to the correct volume. You can also select the correct volume by making use of the titles on the spines of the volumes. At the beginning of each subject, there is a detailed subject index. One useful feature that the third edition has is volumes known as the *Canadian Converters*. These volumes footnote the text with Canadian cases. The fourth edition does not have this feature.

Halsbury's Laws of England (4th Edition)

The fourth edition of *Halsbury's* is the latest edition of the legal encyclopedia. As with the third edition, access to the subject volumes can be had by use of the *General Index* or reference to the spines of the volumes themselves. There are more detailed indexes at the beginning of each subject title. To update a given subject you should begin by consulting the *Cumulative Supplement* which updates the main work with reference to volume and paragraph numbers. There are also *Annual Abridgment* volumes issued each year that outline the development of the law — statutory and case law — and give a listing of periodical articles by subject for the year. Finally there is a looseleaf service, *Current Service*, which has monthly reviews of the law.

Halsbury's is very well respected, and unlike the *C.E.D.*, it is often cited by courts.

LEGAL PERIODICALS

Journal articles and case comments on English law can be accessed through the *Legal Periodical Index, Index to Legal Periodicals,* and *Current Law Index* as well as the *Annual Abridgment* volumes of *Halsbury's.*[1]

LEGAL DICTIONARIES AND WORDS AND PHRASES ENCYCLOPEDIAS

Jowitt's Dictionary of English Law

This is a two volume dictionary. Bound supplements are issued for updating purposes.

Stroud's Judicial Dictionary of Words and Phrases (4th ed.)

This is a five volume set with bound supplements. It makes references to Canadian law as well.

Words and Phrases Legally Defined (2nd ed.)

This five volume set, with bound supplements, has digests of both English and other Commonwealth nations' cases.

Halsbury's Laws of England

Words and phrases can be accessed using the *General Indexes.*

LAW REPORTS

England is the oldest common law jurisdiction in the world and there are reported versions of case law dating from 1220. The earliest reports were written in Law French, not modern English, in the *Year Books.* During the 16th century, private reporters published their own report series known as the *Nominate Reports* because they are named after the various private reporters who published them. There were more than one hundred of these private report series which varied in accuracy and quality. Some cases are reported in more than one Nominate report series. In 1865, report series were established for each court, and the publication of Nominate Report series ceased.

Locating Pre-1865 cases

1. *English Reports, Full Reprint*

---

1 See Chapter Six on how to use periodical indexes.

The *Full Reprint*, contrary to its name, contains a selected number of the early cases from the *Nominate Reports*. There are two index volumes for the 176 volume reporter set. Note that the original pagination of the original *Nominate Reports* is indicated.

2. *Revised Reports*
    The *Revised Reports* contains a selected number of early cases from the *Nominate Reports*. As with the *Full Reprint*, the original pagination of the original *Nominate Reports* is indicated.

3. *All England Law Reports Reprint*
    This reprint contains a selection of earlier cases covering the period from 1558 to 1935.

Law Reports (Cases after 1865)

There are individual Law Report series for each court. Some of these report series can be viewed as topical reports because they deal with a court division that only handles one type of law. For example, the *Family Division Law Reports* contain only Family law cases. Cases can be accessed through the use of cumulative indexes published every ten years. There are also cumulative indexes published on a quarterly basis to cover the current period since the last cumulative index. Cases are listed by name and subject matter. It is also possible to find cases that have considered a certain statute or case.

All England Law Reports

Since 1936, the *All England Law Reports* have been reporting selected cases. In order to access cases, you can use the *Consolidated Tables and Index* which covers 1936 to a recent year. This can be supplemented further by use of the annual *Cumulative Tables and Index* and the bimonthly *Current Cumulative Tables and Index*. Cases are listed by name and subject matter. It is also possible to find cases that have considered a certain statute or case. The *Canadian Supplement* lists cases reported in the *All England Law Reports* that have been cited in reported Canadian cases.

Topical Reports

Topical law reports are available for some English case law. When you are doing research, check to see if you can find a topical law report. Topical law reports are an excellent means to locating relevant case law on your subject area.

THE DIGEST: ANNOTATED BRITISH, COMMONWEALTH, AND EUROPEAN CASES (FORMERLY THE ENGLISH AND EMPIRE DIGEST)

The *Digest* performs the same function for English legal research that the *Canadian Abridgment* performs in the Canadian legal research setting. Case digests are arranged under topics and subtopics and each digest has a paragraph number. The *Digest* also allows you to see the subsequent judicial consideration of the case, since later cases citing the digested case are listed below each digest. The digests are also cross-referenced with *Halsbury's Laws of England.* The *Digest* itself has main volumes supplemented and updated by *Continuation Volumes* and a *Cumulative Supplement.*

To access cases in the *Digest*, you should consult the *Consolidated Index* by searching for a key word or phrase. If you know the name of the case in which you are interested, you may consult the *Consolidated Table of Cases.* To update a given paragraph, you should consult the *Cumulative Supplement* which will indicate any later cases that have considered the case digested in a given paragraph or will list later cases in that subject area. Those later cases can either be found in the *Cumulative Supplement* or one of the *Continuation Volumes.*

NOTING UP ENGLISH CASE LAW

Having found a case(s) on your topic, it is necessary to note it up to see how subsequent cases have considered your case — whether it has been followed, overruled, distinguished, etc.

Cases can be noted up using the *Digest.* Find the paragraph number of the digest of the case that you are updating. Under the digest in the main volume of the *Digest*, you should find a listing of cases that have considered your case. Update this list by checking the *Cumulative Supplement* which will give you a further listing of cases. Digests for the cases listed in this further listing can be found in the *Cumulative Supplement* or one of the *Continuation Volumes.*

STATUTES AND STATUTORY INSTRUMENTS (REGULATIONS)

Your research may require you to look at older statutes or statutes that are currently in force.

Older Statutes

These statutes are contained in three sets. *Statutes of the Realm: 1235-1713; Acts and Ordinances of the Interregnum 1642-1660);* and

Statutes at Large (post 1713). The statutes can be accessed by chronological and subject indexes that accompany the sets.

Statutes Currently in Force

1. *Statutes in Force: Official Revised Edition*
    Statutes currently in force are published in a looseleaf format. Another updating tool is the *Annual Cumulative Supplement* that lists amendments and repeals of Acts with the various subject matter areas.

2. *Halsbury's Statutes of England (4th ed.)*
    This is a bound volume set that can be accessed using the *Consolidated Index*. Statutes can be updated by use of *Cumulative Supplements* and the looseleaf *Noter-up Service*. Using the *Annual Abridgment* of *Halsbury's Laws of England 4th ed.*, you can find useful summaries of the changes to any statute that occurred within the year covered by the *Annual Abridgment* volume that you are consulting.

Regulations

Halsbury's Statutory Instruments

This is a set of volumes containing regulations, in either full text or summary form. The regulations can be accessed by subject in the *Consolidated Index*. To update the main volumes consult the *Annual Supplement* and the *Monthly Survey Summaries* in the *Service Binder*.

You can also find useful summaries of the changes to statutory instruments that occurred within a given year, by consulting the *Annual Abridgment* volume for the year in which you are interested.

19

American Legal Research

INTRODUCTION

This chapter, while not a detailed statement on American legal research, will outline how to use the key American legal research tools.[1] The chapter will be of use for those doing American legal research for the purpose of a Canadian research problem. American law is never binding in Canada. Canadian researchers will, however, find American legal research to be helpful when the law on the area they are researching has not been well developed in Canada or is in a state of confusion. In these circumstances, the analysis and rationale underlying American case law may be persuasive in Canada. A study on the extent to which the Supreme Court of Canada refers to foreign law in its judgments found that seventy-five percent of such references were to American decisions.[2]

APPROACHING AMERICAN LEGAL RESEARCH

Our approach to American legal research is the same as our approach to Canadian legal research. We recommend that you begin your research by consulting secondary sources such as legal encyclopedias, treatises, periodicals, and looseleafs. These sources will refer you to the leading cases and relevant statutes on your topic and provide an interpretive guide of the law. We then recommend a more detailed analysis of your topic through the use of topical law reports and digests or both. Your final step is to note up the case and statutory law you have found.

THE AMERICAN COURT STRUCTURE

When doing American legal research, it is essential that you have an understanding of the American court structure. The persuasiveness of legal principles derived from American decisions will depend, in part, on the level of court.

---

1 For a more detailed discussion of American legal research, see Cohen & Olson, *Legal Research in a Nutshell* (St. Paul, Minn.: West Publishing Co., 1991); or Wren & Wren, *The Legal Research Manual* 2nd ed. (Madison, Wisconsin: Adams & Ambrose Publishing, 1986).

2 Casswell, "Doctrine and Foreign Law in the Supreme Court of Canada: A Quantitative Analysis" (1981), 2 *Supreme Court L.R.* 435.

The United States has a dual court system: federal and state. In the federal system, there are three court levels: (1) U.S. District Courts; (2) U.S. Court of Appeals; and (3) the U.S. Supreme Court. The U.S. District Courts are trial courts which deal with matters falling under the federal government's jurisdiction. Every state is divided into one or more federal districts. The U.S. Court of Appeals are the court of first appeal from District Courts. The U.S. Supreme Court is the highest court of appeal at the federal level.

The state system consists of either two or three levels of court, depending on the state. Where three levels exist, they are:

1. Trial Courts (may be called County Court, District Court, Superior Court, etc.) and Speciality Courts (includes Civil Court, Family Court, Probate Court, etc.)
2. Court of first Appeals (usually called [state] Court of Appeal)
3. Court of final Appeals (usually called [state] Supreme Court)

Those states that have only two levels of court do not have the intermediate appeal court or Court of First Appeals. Different states refer to the three levels of state courts differently. For instance, in New York state, the trial court is called the Supreme Court, the court of first appeal is called Supreme Court Appellate Division, and the court of final appeal is called the Court of Appeal. In contrast, in Delaware, the trial court is called the Superior Court, the court of first appeal is called the Court of Chancery, and the court of final appeal is called the Supreme Court.

When using American cases for the purpose of a Canadian legal research problem, you should focus primarily on decisions from the Supreme Court or the U.S. Court of Appeals. However, there are some instances when state law can be persuasive. For example, the corporate commercial law of Delaware is highly influential in Canada.

LEGAL ENCYCLOPEDIAS

Corpus Juris Secundum **(West Publishing Company)**

The *Corpus Juris Secundum* ("*C.J.C.*") is an encyclopedia of American law consisting of roughly 150 volumes organized alphabetically by subject. Every chapter or subject title contains a detailed table of contents and a "scope note". The "scope note", which precedes the discussion of the law on the topic, outlines what is covered in the chapter and where related topics can be found. A five volume "General Index" facilitates access to the subject titles.

The General Index and subject volumes are updated with cumulative pocket supplements. The *C.J.C.* covers federal and state law and attempts to cite all relevant reported cases in footnotes.

American Jurisprudence 2nd (Lawyer's Cooperative Publishing Company)

American Jurisprudence 2nd ("*American Jurisprudence*") is an encyclopedia of American law consisting of roughly eighty volumes organized alphabetically by subject. A multi-volume index also facilitates access to the subject or title volumes. Each chapter or subject title contains a detailed table of contents. All chapters begin with a "scope paragraph", which defines what is covered in the chapter, and cross references to other chapters dealing with additional aspects of the subject. The index and title volumes are kept up-to-date by pocket supplements and by a looseleaf binder entitled *Am. Jur. 2d New Topic Service*.

American Jurisprudence covers federal and state law. Unlike the *C.J.C.*, *American Jurisprudence* does not attempt to cite all reported cases in footnotes. Citations are to *American Law Reports* (discussed below) annotations and to United States Supreme Court decisions.

American Jurisprudence Proof of Facts 2nd (Lawyer's Cooperative Publishing Company)

American Jurisprudence Proof of Facts 2nd ("*Proof of Facts*") is a multi-volume encyclopedia for litigators on how to go about proving facts at trial. This publication was designed to assist lawyers in preparing for examination-in-chief and cross-examination. However, it will also be useful in preparing for discoveries and interviews with clients and witnesses.

Each subject covered is divided into three main parts. The first part ("prefatory material") includes a concise statement of the fact-in-issue. The second part ("background text") sets out law applicable to the fact situation. Substantive law is discussed to the extent that it is necessary for a proper understanding of the "proofs". However, there is a table at the beginning of each chapter which cross references the treatment of substantive law in *American Jurisprudence* to the proofs in *Proof of Facts*. The third part ("proofs") is question and answer interchanges between lawyers and witnesses. Where not readily apparent, the purpose of particular questions or lines of questioning are explained. Suggested answers are given to alert lawyers to the type of information that must be obtained from the witness. Textual notes containing evidentiary rules and practical suggestions for questioning witnesses are included.

Proof of Facts is organized alphabetically by subject, and a multi-volume index facilitates access to the various subject or title volumes. The index is kept up-to-date with periodic pocket supplements.

American Law Reports ("A.L.R.")

The *A.L.R.* is a several hundred volume series of encyclopedia-like books which annotate a selected number of cases in given subject areas. The reported case or a summary thereof (few cases are reported in full) precedes the annotation. Next, the subject of the annotation is defined (e.g., directors liability). While the case may deal with several legal issues, the annotation may only cover one of them. Often there is a table of contents, a table of jurisprudence cross-references, and a paragraph defining the scope of the annotation. The actual annotations summarize the case law on the subject, attempt to reconcile conflicting decisions, and assess which cases are binding and why.

The *A.L.R. Federal* covers federal law, whereas the *A.L.R.* 3rd covers mainly state law. The "Quick Index" permits access to the *A.L.R.* and *A.L.R. Federal*. Bound Quick Index volumes are updated with pocket supplements.

The researcher should be aware that the *A.L.R.* 3rd and 4th, and *A.L.R. Federal* are not as comprehensive in their coverage of the law as West's Digest discussed below. However, unlike *A.L.R.* 3rd and *A.L.R. Federal*, *West's Digest* does not contain explanatory notes or attempt to reconcile conflicting decisions.

RESTATEMENTS OF THE LAW

Restatements of the Law ("Restatements"), published by the American Law Institute, provide concise statements of the common law rules on various topics. Each chapter includes "black letter" statements of law, followed by commentary and explanatory notes. There are Restatements on ten main subject areas: agency; conflict of laws; contracts; foreign relations law; judgments; property; restitution; security; torts; and trusts.

Restatements are very respected secondary literature and often cited in American court decisions to summarize the law in an area. *Restatements in the Courts* annotates the court decisions which have applied or interpreted the various sections of the Restatements.

LEGAL PERIODICALS

Journal articles and case comments on American law can be accessed through the *Index to Legal Periodicals* and *Current Law Index*.[3]

---

3 Chapter Six on Legal Periodicals outlines how to use these indexes.

LEGAL DICTIONARIES AND WORDS AND PHRASES ENCYCLOPEDIAS

The most widely used American legal dictionaries are: *Black's Law Dictionary* 6th ed. (West Publishing Co., 1992) and *Ballentine's Law Dictionary, with Pronunciations* 3rd ed.(Lawyers' Cooperative Publishing Co., 1969). As can be seen, *Black's Law Dictionary* is considerably more up-to-date.

Words and Phrases (West Publishing Co.) is the most comprehensive words and phrases encyclopedia. There are roughly 50 volumes, organized alphabetically and updated annually with pocket supplements found at the back of each volume. *Words and Phrases* purports to list all cases that have offered judicial consideration of a word or phrase.

LAW REPORTS

There are federal and state law reports, in additon to law reports which digest decisions, based on the level of court in which the case was decided, the region of the country, and the subject area.

One of the best ways of locating cases on your topic, after having consulted legal encyclopedias, periodicals, and treatises to obtain an overview of the topic, is by using the subject indexes of the topical law reports.[4]

DIGESTS

Digests, like the *Canadian Abridgment*, enable you to find cases under your subject. West Publishing Company's *American Digest System* is the most comprehensive American digest and facilitates access to almost all reported American case law. The system consists of a series of digests which divides all American fields of law into over four hundred topics. Every topic is further divided into numerous subtopics. Subtopics are identified by: (*a*) the name of the topic under which they fall, and (*b*) a key number that designates their specific subdivision within the topic.

West writes a one sentence headnote or "squib" for each point of law in every case it receives. Every headnote is numbered, and the same number will appear in the reported decision where the point of law is discussed. A topic name and key number is given to each headnote to identify its substance. The Digests bring together all headnotes with the same topic name and key number. You should note that there are no explanatory notes and that the headnotes do not attempt to reconcile conflicting decisions.

---

4 See Appendix I for a selective list of American topical law reports.

West publishes a number of digests which gather headnotes from different regions or jurisdictions. The *American Digest System* is known as a master index to all U.S. case law.

American Digest System

Volumes of the *American Digest* are issued regularly in a series called the *General Digest*. Each volume gathers under topic and key number all of the squibs written in any of the reporters since the last volume. Since 1976 the *General Digest* has been consolidated and republished every five years. Prior to 1976 consolidations were done every ten years. A multi-volume index facilitates access to the subject volumes.

There are three main ways of locating case law on your topic using the *General Digest*.

Descriptive Word Approach

1. The Descriptive-Word Index is arranged alphabetically. It includes all topics of the digest classification, descriptive words relating to the parties to the action, the names of places and physical objects, questions of law, legal principles, and constitutional and legislative provisions.

2. When looking for your topic under the Descriptive-Word Index, start with a very specific word or phrase that denotes the question you must answer. Try to think of the least common denominator to your research problem. If you cannot find anything under this very specific entry, try a slightly broader topic until you find something on point. Avoid broad subject headings such as "damages" or "injunctions", as you will find too many entries, most of which will be irrelevant to your topic.

3. Once you have located an appropriate descriptive word or phrase, you will be referred to a corresponding digest topic and key number.

4. Locate the volume containing your topic in the *General Digest* and consolidations. You will find paragraph case summaries under the digest topics and citations for the cases.

5. Read the case summaries and look up the actual cases when they look relevant to your facts.

Topic Approach

Only use this approach if you have a strong knowledge of the law on your topic, as it is very easy to miss important aspects of your topic by selecting incorrect topic and key numbers.

1. Scan the list of topics which you will find in each Digest volume for the appropriate topic name.

2. Locate the volume containing your topic in the *General Digest* and consolidations. You will find a "scope note" under the topic name in the *General Digest*. This note outlines what is included in the topic and provides the various sub-topics and key numbers. Since the same key numbers are used throughout the West system, every case on the topic can be located.

3. Read the case summaries under the digest topics and look up the actual cases when they look relevant to your facts.

Case Name Approach

1. If you know the name and citation of a case on your topic, you can locate the case in the *West Reporter* and obtain the relevant key number from the headnote.
    ALTERNATIVELY, you can locate the case in the Table of Cases in the *General Digest*. Cases are listed alphabetically, along with their citations and the topic and key number for each point of law drawn from the case.[5]

2. Locate the volume containing your topic in the *General Digest* and consolidations.

3. Read the case summaries under the digest topics and look up the actual cases when they look relevant to your facts.

The *American Digest System* can be time-consuming to use due to the number of decisions digested. The researcher will find it necessary to read many irrelevant entries before locating the citations she or he requires. In addition, changes in statutory or case law, unless mentioned in the headnote, are not indicated. For these reasons, where possible, we would recommend using the topical reports over this system.

Other Digests

While the *American Digest System* is a master digest for the entire country, there are more specialized digests for particular regions of the country,[6] for individual states, and for particular courts.[7] These digests are

---

5 The Table of Cases also includes the case history of each decision if such information was available when the Table was prepared.

6 The Regional Digests are: *Atlantic Digest, Northwestern Digest, Pacific Digest, Southeastern Digest,* and *Southern Digest*.

7 Court digests include: *Federal Practice Digest 2d, United States Supreme Court Reports Digest,* and *United States Supreme Court Digest*. Topical digests for other federal courts include: *West's Bankruptcy Digest, Military Reporter Digest, U.S. Court of Claims Digest, West's Federal Case News,* and *Tax Cases*.

useful when you know that you only need to find case law from a particular state or region or from a particular court. As these digests are not as comprehensive as the *American Digest System*, they are less time consuming to use.

NOTING UP AMERICAN CASE LAW

Once you have found a case(s) on your topic, you must always note it up. This will ensure that the case still stands for the law — ie., it has not been overturned. It will also let you know how the case has been considered, distinguished, applied, etc.

Shepard's Citation Service allows you to follow the history of your case and to determine the judicial treatment of the case. Shepard's Citators list virtually every published and unpublished case by case citation (ie., reporter, volume and page number; the name of the case is not included). Articles and case comments which have considered the case are also cited.

The term "shepardize" a case means to note-up the case. When the case you are shepardizing has been cited in more than one law report, alternative citations are usually given in brackets. Below each citation of the case, you will find listed the citations of all cases which have considered the case and an abbreviation representing the way in which the case was considered. For example, "a" means the same case was affirmed on appeal, "r" means the same case was reversed on appeal, and "d" means the case at bar is different, either in law or fact, from the case cited for reasons provided. Check the front of the volume of the Citator you are using for an up-to-date and thorough list of abbreviations and their meanings.

There are different volumes of *Shepard Citators* for different law reports. To shepardize a case, you must begin by finding the *Shepard Citator* which covers cases in the law reporter where your case is digested. You must also ensure that you locate the Citator which covers the volume of the law reporter where your case is digested. Bound volumes of *Shepard Citators* cover decisions reported in a given law report over a specified number of years. For instance, one Citator may cover volumes 1 through 60 of a given law reporter, whereas another Citator may cover volumes 61 through 120. You will find the citation of the case under the volume and page number of the case. Bound volumes of Shepard Citators are kept up-to-date by means of periodically published hard and softcover supplements.

STATUTES

Federal Statutes

A federal bill becomes a statute after being passed by both houses of Congress and being signed by the President.

New statutes first become available in *U.S. Code Congressional and Administrative News Service* (West Publishing Co.) and *United States Code Service, Lawyers' Edition* (Lawyers' Cooperative Publishing Co.). At the end of each two year congressional session, statutes are published in numerical sequence in the *United States Statutes at Large*. The *United States Code* (the "*Code*") is a consolidation of American federal statutes that is published every six years. Cumulative Supplements are published to update the *Code*.

There are also two privately published editions of the *Code*:
1. *United States Code Annotated* (West Publishing Co.); and
2. *United States Code Service, Lawyers' Edition* (Lawyers Cooperative Publishing Co.).

These two publications are annotated and cite cases that consider the various sections of the statute. Both annotated editions of the *Code* are updated with annual pocket parts, monthly pamphlet supplements, and reissue of volumes when necessary.

State Statutes

Statutes are published in session laws, similar to the *U.S. Statutes at Large*, at the end of state legislative sessions. The titles of the publications consolidating state laws differ from state to state. Often the titles of consolidations of state statutes will use the words "code", "consolidated", "compiled", or "revised".

Most states also have annotated Code services similar to those described above for federal statutes.

Uniform Laws

Uniform laws are laws which are intended to apply to all states so as to minimize the confusion created by unnecessarily different laws, particularly in the area of trade and commerce. The *Uniform Commercial Code* is perhaps the best known unified law. As each state is legislatively autonomous, before a uniform law will apply to any given state, it must be enacted by that state.

Uniform laws are published in *Uniform Laws Annotated* (West Publishing Co.). This publication includes tables specifying which states have adopted each law and any variations in the form in which they have been adopted. *Uniform Laws Annotated* is updated with pocket supplements.[8]

---

8 The *Martindale-Hubbell Law Directory* also contains the text of uniform laws. For a more detailed description of this directory, refer to Chapter Seventeen.

Appendix I

Selective List of American Topical Law Reports

Abortion Law Reporter (National Abortion Rights Action League)
Accounting Law Reports (CCH)
Administrative Law Service (Pike & Fischer)
Aviation Law Reports (CCH)
Bankruptcy Court Decisions (Corporate Reorganization Reporter Inc.)
Bankruptcy Law Reports (CCH)
Blue Sky Law Reports (CCH)
Class Action Reporter (Plus Publications, Inc.)
Common Market Reports (CCH)
Copyright Law Reporter (CCH)
Criminal Law Reporter (Bureau of National Affairs, Inc.)
Energy Management (CCH)
Entertainment Law Reporter (E.L.R. Publishing Co.)
Ethics in Government Reporter (Washington Service Bureau)
Environment Reporter (Bureau of National Affairs, Inc.)
Environmental Law Reporter (Environmental Law Institute)
Family Law Reporter (Bureau of National Affairs, Inc.)
Federal Banking Law Reports (CCH)
Federal Securities Law Reports (CCH)
Fire and Casualty Insurance Law Reports (CCH)
Housing and Development Reporter (Bureau of National Affairs, Inc.)
Indian Law Reporter (Amer. Indian Lawyer Training Program)
Inheritance, Estate & Gift Tax Reports (CCH)
International Environment Reporter (Bureau of National Affairs, Inc.)
International Trade Reporter (Bureau of National Affairs, Inc.)
Job Safety and Health Reporter (Business Publishers Inc.)
Labor Arbitration Awards (CCH)
Labor Arbitration Reports (Bureau of National Affairs, Inc.)
Labor Relations Reporter (Bureau of National Affairs, Inc.)
Land Development Law Reporter (Land Development Institute Ltd.)
Life, Health and Accident Law Reports (CCH)
Media Law Reporter (Bureau of National Affairs, Inc.)
Mental Disability Law Reporter (American Bar Association)
Military Law Reporter (Public Law Education Institute)
Noise Regulation Reporter (Bureau of National Affairs, Inc.)
Pension Reporter (Bureau of National Affairs, Inc.)
Poverty Law Reports (CCH)
Product Liability Reports (CCH)

Product Safety and Liability Reporter (Bureau of National Affairs, Inc.)
Professional Liability Reporter (Prof. Liability Rptr. Co.)
Search and Seizure Law Report (Clark Boardman Company, Ltd.)
Securities and Federal Corporate Law Report (Clark Boardman Company
    Ltd.)
Securities Regulation & Law Report (Bureau of National Affairs, Inc.)
Trade Regulations Reports (CCH)
Tax Court Decisions Reports (CCH)
Tax Court Reports (CCH)
Uniform Commercial Code Reporting Service (Callaghan & Company)
Union Labor Report (Bureau of National Affairs, Inc.)
White Collar Report (Bureau of National Affairs, Inc.)
Women's Rights Law Reporter (Rutgers Law School)
Workmen's Compensation Law Reports (CCH)

20

Guidelines for Writing: Legal Essays, Case Comments and Legal Memoranda

This chapter will offer guidelines on writing legal essays, case comments, and legal memoranda. The focus of the chapter is on legal memoranda, and Appendix I to this chapter contains a sample legal memorandum. We have chosen legal memoranda for our focus because if you article it is guaranteed that you will be required to write numerous legal memoranda and many students will have never seen or written a legal memorandum when they begin their articles. Further, legal memoranda are not published. In contrast, examples of essays and case comments are readily available in law journals.

GENERAL COMMENTS

Writing Style

A discussion of grammar and writing style is beyond the scope of this chapter. Suffice it to say that poor grammar and writing style will confuse the reader. Complex sentence structures and a verbose writing style should be avoided. A simple, easy-to-read style is infinitely more effective.[1]

Organization

An effective piece of legal writing will be organized in a logical manner that is easy to follow and understand. Inappropriate organization can mislead the reader and obscure the legal argument and analysis.

Two things should drive the organization scheme that you choose for your written work: the subject matter and your audience. Each subject matter tends to have its own logic. An understanding of what this logic is, will assist you in finding the most rational places to put headings and subheadings. The use of headings will make your document more user-friendly. In organizing your document, you should also keep in mind your audience's interests and level of understanding. For example, a paper on recent amendments to the *Ontario Labour Relations Act*, written for a

---

1 See e.g., Perrin, *Better Writing for Lawyers* (Toronto: Law Society of Upper Canada, 1990) and Rooke, *A Grammar Booklet for Lawyers* (Toronto: Law Society of Upper Canada, 1991).

non-legal private sector audience, would be different from a paper written for a strictly legal audience.

Use of Gender Neutral Language

Historically the masculine gender has been assumed to be the norm. This is evidenced by terms such as "mankind", "manpower", "layman", and the use of "he" as a generic pronoun. The inherent gender bias in our language is inconsistent with the goal of achieving equality between the sexes in the workplace and in society. Accordingly, we recommend always using gender neutral language in your legal writing. If you find it awkward or clumsy to constantly repeat the pronouns "he or she", you can use plurals or alternate between using the masculine and feminine pronoun.

LEGAL ESSAYS

There are many types of legal essays. For instance, an essay may do one or more of the following:
- report on trends in an area of law and speculate on future developments;
- suggest reforms to the existing law;
- apply a theoretical framework to an area of law;
- examine the law from an historical perspective; or
- compare the law in different jurisdictions.

The parameters of a legal essay are generally left to the author's discretion. The introduction to your paper should clearly define these parameters. You should consider the parameters in terms of subject matter, jurisdiction, and time frame. Other parameters, depending on your topic, may be relevant. Sometimes, it will also be necessary to justify the parameters you have chosen. If you define your parameters and provide adequate justification for them, you will insulate yourself from unfair criticism. Further, your introduction should identify the purpose of the paper and your thesis.

An important principle of essay writing is to never assume that your readers possess an in depth knowledge of the topic. Whether your essay is understandable should not be dependent on the expertise of your readers. A number of implications follow from this principle.

You should begin by defining and/or describing any other terms, concepts, or theories which are not common knowledge. For instance, if your analysis is based on economic theory, state the basic principles of this theory and any assumptions the theory makes. If your paper is about the regulation of a certain industry or market (e.g., the construction industry or securities market), you may also have to describe the special conditions which give rise to such regulation. This will enable the reader to understand and evaluate your analysis.

First, after your introduction, you should always begin by outlining what the existing law is on your topic.[2] For an essay to be comprehensible, a description of the existing law is essential background. All of your subsequent comments about trends in the law, reforms, or theories will only make sense in relation to your presentation of the existing law. For instance, you cannot write a logical and effective essay proposing reforms to the rape shield law before you first set out what the law is on the subject. The rationale underlying your proposed reforms will not be clear. Failure to outline your understanding and assumptions as to the current state of the law will also confuse the reader who is not familiar with the law. Even readers who are familiar with the topic will not have the benefit of seeing how you understand the existing law, and consequently they may misconstrue your analysis.

It is important to present the précis of the law in a separate section. Do not try to describe the existing law intermingled with your analytic comments as this will confuse the reader. Other sections of the essay may describe, for instance, the problems with the current law prompting the need for reform, the nature of the proposed reform, and the implications of such reform or how a legal theory applies.

When discussing the law on your topic, you should always be balanced and thorough in your treatment of it. Do not gloss over or neglect to mention cases which do not support your thesis. Tackle any discrepancies directly. Further, you should be critical of your own position and attempt to anticipate and neutralize counter-arguments.

The conclusion of your essay should reiterate your purpose and thesis, and indicate how the paper has satisfied these by summarizing your analysis and arguments. Often you will want to suggest questions for further research in your conclusion.

CASE COMMENTS

A case comment describes and critically analyzes a judicial decision. When selecting a case on which to comment, you should choose a case which has a controversial aspect and which signals and/or clarifies the direction of the law.

The introduction of a case comment should describe in general terms the subject matter of the case. As with a legal essay, you should define the parameters of your comment. For instance, if the case covers several areas

---

2 You may find that the general principles, outlined in Chapter Two, are helpful for gaining an understanding of the existing law in a subject-area.

of law and you only wish to focus your comment on one area, make this explicit. The judicial history of the case (i.e., how the case was decided in lower courts) may also be something you wish to outline in your introduction. However, sometimes the judicial history will be so important that you will wish to discuss it in greater detail in the body of the comment. In addition, you may wish to briefly outline your assessment of the case, or what you intend to argue with respect to the case, in the introduction. What are the implications of the decision? Does the case represent a beneficial or potentially harmful development in the law?

When writing a case comment, you should generally begin by outlining the facts and the reasoning of the case. Next, your comment should attempt to answer one or more of the following questions:

1. How does this case affect the existing law on the topic?
2. What are the implications of the case for the future?
3. Does this case typify a trend that can or cannot be traced in other jurisdictions?

When analyzing the case and the law in the area, you should always be balanced and thorough, despite any interpretation you may favour. Do not gloss over or neglect to mention arguments or law that is inconsistent with your interpretation. Be critical of your own arguments.

Your conclusion should summarize your analysis of the case and comment on future implications.

LEGAL MEMORANDA

The purpose of a legal memorandum is to answer a legal question(s) in the context of a specific set of facts. The parameters of a legal memorandum are generally more narrow than those of an essay. In essays, it can be desirable and interesting to discuss issues of policy, legal reform, legal theory and comparative law or both. In fact, it is a discussion of these matters which often set high quality papers apart from mediocre ones. In contrast, legal theory, legal reform, policy, and comparative law are generally outside the scope of a legal memorandum. A legal memorandum should only contain that information which is necessary to answer the question(s) it has set out to assess. You are not concerned with what the law *should be*, unless you have been specifically asked to address law reform issues. Instead, your mandate is to outline what the law is and to discuss its impact on your client's case. Ultimately, the lawyer assigning the memorandum will have to advise the client about a particular course of action. That advice may be based, in part, on what your memorandum recommends. An effective memorandum should, therefore, contain a thorough analysis of the relevant law and provide a well-reasoned answer to the question posed.

Organization of a Legal Memorandum

We have outlined a structure which will help to ensure that your memorandum is focused and organized. This is a structure which is commonly used throughout the legal profession. The proposed structure contains seven main headings: Issues; Short Answer; The Facts; The Law; Analysis; Conclusion; and List of Authorities. The purpose and contents of each of these headings are described below.

While we feel that this structure will serve in the vast majority of situations, the structure of your memorandum should ultimately be dictated by the logic of your subject matter and the needs of your audience.

Issues[3]

This section of the memorandum should outline the issue(s) you have been asked to analyze. The issues should be framed in terms of questions which you will ultimately answer.

The assigning lawyer may frame the legal issues for you. Alternatively, she or he may simply outline the factual context and problem(s) confronting the client(s), leaving you to determine the relevant legal issues. In either case, it is imperative that you understand clearly what the question(s) is that you have been asked to answer. Otherwise your research will be unfocused and you will waste time in the library. If you are unsure, confirm the instructions with the assigning lawyer. You are well advised to do this before beginning your research, as the questions will rarely become more obvious after hours in the library.

Often, once you begin your research, you will identify sub-issues which are critical to an analysis of the central issues that the assigning lawyer has set out. While it is crucial that you comprehend what the central issues or questions are when you begin your research, you should keep in mind that the definition of the issues and particularly sub-issues is an ongoing process.

The sequence of issues can also be important. It is usually preferable to deal with the central issues first. Always ensure that there is a logical connection between successive issues and sub-issues.

Short Answer

The short answer section of the memorandum is a summary of your conclusions. It is useful to set out such a summary at the beginning so that the assigning lawyer has a sense of where your analysis is going. This

---

3 Refer to the discussion of the "Description of the Issues" section of the Checklist in Chapter Three.

section also forces the writer to be disciplined and to answer the question(s) posed. The answer should not be wishy-washy. It should be a "yes" or a "no", and it should be predicated on a balanced and thorough analysis of the law as applied to your facts. This section is only meant to contain a brief summary of your analysis.

The Facts

This section will set out the factual context in which you have been asked to assess a legal problem(s). It is important that you give a detailed description of the *relevant* facts so that the assigning lawyer can see from what facts you are drawing your conclusions. Facts which are not relevant to the issues you have been asked to assess need not be cited.

If you have been given insufficient facts to analyze and answer the question properly, be sure to ask for additional information or review the file yourself. Often, once you have begun your research of the law, you will realize that further facts are needed to analyze the problem properly. It is preferable to ask for additional information before submitting the memorandum than to be asked to supplement the memorandum at a later date.

The Law

This section of the memorandum outlines the *relevant* statutory and case law on the question(s) you have been asked to analyze. As discussed above, a legal memorandum is different from a law school essay or journal article. The sole purpose of a legal memorandum is to answer one or more usually very specific questions. Therefore, information that might be interesting to include in an essay, such as a critique of the law and an examination of how the law could be reformed, will be irrelevant to a memorandum if it does not help to answer the question(s) posed. Before including law in your memorandum, always ask yourself how this law helps you to answer the question(s) posed.

The length of this section of the memorandum will depend on the complexity of the legal issue(s) you have been asked to assess. Sometimes the answer to your question may be set out in a statute. If this is the case, you may only have to determine how the relevant statutory provision has been judicially considered to complete this section of the memorandum. Where there is not a statute that answers your question, you will want to examine the case law in your jurisdiction. When citing a case in support of a general, well-established proposition of law, it is sufficient to cite one or two recent cases decided by appellate courts. On more controversial matters, a more extensive use of case law will be necessary.

Where there is no case law on point in your jurisdiction, you will want to research case law on your topic in other jurisdictions in Canada, preferably decisions from appellate courts. While these decisions would not be binding in your jurisdiction, the rationale underlying them may prove persuasive.[4] Finally, where there is no Canadian law on your research problem, or where the Canadian law is in a state of confusion, it may be useful to draw on American and British law or both. Decisions from these countries may also prove persuasive in your jurisdiction.

Your description of the law must be thorough and balanced. Be sure to include any cases which go against the answer you or the assigning lawyer hope to reach. If the law is in a state of confusion, say so and try to summarize, as clearly as possible, where the confusion or conflict exists.

It can be helpful to quote from cases. The assigning lawyer will often want to know precisely how the court frames or defines legal propositions. As a general rule, however, avoid long quotations, and only quote that which is necessary to make your point. When quoting from a case, give the judge's name and the page number from which the quotation is drawn. Where applicable, also indicate if the judge is writing for a unanimous court or for the majority, or if the judge is writing a concurring or dissenting opinion. Even when you are not using a quotation and are just stating the law as it is enunciated in a case, it is still a good practice to indicate relevant page numbers, the judge's name, and whether or not the judge is writing for a unanimous court, the majority, or a concurring or dissenting judgment.

Law can be cited in the body of the memorandum or in footnotes. Do not use endnotes, as they are more time-consuming to read. Follow the rules for legal citation set out in the *Canadian Guide to Uniform Legal Citation* 2nd ed. (the "McGill Guide").[5]

If you have been asked to analyze more than one legal issue, use separate headings for each issue. Separate headings make the memorandum easier to follow and promote an organized style. If each legal issue can be further broken down into subtopics, separate these topics with the use of subheadings. The layout of the legal issues in this section should parallel the way issues are set out in the first section of the memorandum.

Analysis

In this section, the facts are applied to the law to answer the question. Your analysis should follow the sequence set out in the "issues" and "law" sections of the memorandum.

You will rarely find a case that is identical to the one you are researching. Most legal problems which you will be asked to analyze will fall into gaps between decided cases. Your task is to form legal arguments that

---

4 Refer to the flow chart in Chapter Two on distinguishing between binding and persuasive law and prioritizing the various sources of law.

5 Toronto: Carswell, 1988.

interpolate or extrapolate from the principles of decided cases. The following are questions you should address in this section of the memorandum:

1. Based on the law, does the client have a case?
2. What are the strengths and weaknesses of the case?
3. Is the law which supports or goes against your client's case binding or persuasive?
4. Can the facts of your case be distinguished from those in the case law? If so, how?
5. Will a court be likely to accept these distinctions as valid? Why or why not?

Conclusions

This section should summarize your analysis and answer the question(s) set out in the "Issues" section of the memorandum.

Your answer to the question(s) should be as categorical as possible. The assigning lawyer is relying on you to advise him or her. An inconclusive answer will be of little assistance. Your answer should be supported by reasons written in general terms.

List of Authorities

This section includes a numerical listing of all secondary sources which you consulted. The list will ensure the assigning lawyer that you have been thorough in your research.

Alternative Format

An alternative method to the one described above will combine the "Law" and "Analysis" sections into one section entitled "Analysis" or "Discussion". The advantage of this style is that you will avoid some of the repetition inevitable in the above method. We recommend using this style when you are analyzing several legal issues. The memorandum will often be easier to follow if you complete your discussion of both the law and analysis of an issue before delving into another conceptually distinct legal issue. As with the above format, we recommend the frequent use of headings and subheadings so that the memorandum is organized and easy to understand.

Appendix I

A SAMPLE LEGAL MEMORANDUM

MEMORANDUM

To: Student
From: Lawyer
Re: Green v. Brown
File#: 111222
Date: August 17, 1992

Our client, Green, entered a written contract of employment with Brown for an indefinite term under which Green would manage Brown's car dealership. Brown drafted the contract and our client had her lawyer review the agreement. Just prior to signing the agreement, there were last minute negotiations which resulted in handwritten changes to the contract. Our client did not receive legal advice with respect to the changes that were initiated by Brown. Ten months after the agreement was signed, Brown dismissed Green without just cause. There is now a dispute between Green and Brown, over the compensation to which Green is entitled under the terms of the agreement.

The contract contained the following clauses. The phrases appearing in italics are the handwritten additions to the contract:

Paragraph 3:
>In the event that the Employee is terminated for reasons other than just cause, she or he is entitled to base salary *plus $15,000.*

Paragraph 8:
>The Dealership agrees to provide the following remuneration package: . . . (ii) a bonus calculated according to the terms set out in the Dealership's Manager Bonus Plan *with a minimum annual guarantee of $15,000.*

Our client, who took detailed notes during the discussions just prior to the signing of the contract, maintains that she is entitled to her base salary plus $15,000 and a bonus of $19,000 calculated under the Manager Bonus Plan. She says that this interpretation was made very clear in the discussions. According to our client, the two references to "$15,000" in the contract are to two different entitlements.

Brown maintains that the two references to "$15,000" are to the same entitlement, meaning that our client is only entitled to her base salary plus $15,000.

The situation involves problems of contractual interpretation. I would like you to research the law with respect to the admissibility of parol evidence. Can we introduce Brown's evidence about the discussions that occurred just before the contract was signed? Further, if we can introduce such evidence, can we persuade a court to apply the doctrine of *contra proferentum*, interpreting the contract against the author, in favour of our client.

MEMORANDUM

To: Lawyer
From: Student
Re: Green v. Brown
File #: 111222
Date: August 21, 1992

ISSUES

You have asked me to research the following questions:
(1) What is the test for admissibility of parol evidence?; and
(2) Under what circumstances do courts apply the doctrine of *contra proferentum?*

SHORT ANSWER

Parol Evidence

If there is ambiguity in a contract, parol evidence can be admitted to explain it, provided the interpretation is not contradictory of the terms of the contract. Mere difficulty of interpretation does not constitute ambiguity. Authorities conflict about whether parol evidence can be used to establish the presence of ambiguity.

In our case there seems to be latent ambiguity on the face of the contract. Our client asserts that mention of $15,000 refers to different entitlements, while the defendant interprets all mentions of $15,000, as being to the same entitlement. This is not a matter of difficulty of interpretation, and parol evidence is not necessary to establish the presence of ambiguity. Accordingly, we should be able to succeed in having the parol evidence admitted.

Contra Proferentum

If there is ambiguity in a contract, the doctrine of *contra proferentum* can be used to interpret the ambiguous clause against the author. The rule is applied where the party pleading it had no opportunity to modify the wording.

Our facts satisfy the precondition of ambiguity; however, there may be a problem with respect to the condition that the person relying on the doctrine has not had an opportunity to modify the clause. Given that the impugned sections were modified just prior to signing, there is the suggestion that our client had some opportunity to modify the contract. Parol evidence would be needed to establish that the clauses were imposed on our client by the defendant. There is no case law equating lack of independent legal advice with respect to contractual changes as being equivalent to lacking an opportunity to modify the contract. If the doctrine of *contra proferentum* is interpreted as a response to inequality of bargaining power, we may have an argument. Overall there is some doubt about whether we can meet the test for use of *contra proferentum*.

FACTS

Our client, Green, entered an employment contract with Brown to manage a car dealership. Green had the contract, which was drafted by Brown, reviewed by her lawyer. At the meeting to sign the agreement, Green agreed to a few handwritten changes to the agreement which were not reviewed by her lawyer. Green kept detailed notes about the meeting. After ten months, Green was dismissed without just cause.

The contract contained two clauses, both of which contain handwritten references to the sum "$15,000". Paragraph 2 of the contract sets out a formula for Green's remuneration upon termination without just cause as being base salary plus $15,000. The "plus $15,000" was a handwritten addition. Paragraph 8 of the contract sets out Green's bonus entitlements as being those calculated under the Manager Bonus Plan with a minimum annual guarantee of $15,000. The "minimum annual guarantee of $15,000" was a handwritten addition. Green now claims that she is entitled to her base salary plus $15,000, and a bonus calculated under the plan equal to $19,000. Her understanding of the contract is based on the discussion that took place just before the contract was signed. Brown maintains that Green's remuneration upon termination does not include the bonus because the reference in Paragraph 8 to $15,000 was to the same entitlement as the reference to $15,000 in Paragraph 3.

LAW

The Parol Evidence Rule

The general rule with respect to contracts is that the court is confined to considering the written agreement in interpreting the contract and will not consider extrinsic evidence. However, if there is ambiguity, the court can admit parol evidence to explain the terms of the contract.

As Cory J.A. stated for the court in *TransCanada Pipelines v. Northern & Central Gas Corp.* (1983), 146 D.L.R. (3d) 293 at 296 (Ont. C.A.):

> Trite as it may be, it is appropriate to begin by repeating the well-known rule that where parties have set out the terms of their contract in a written document, as a general rule, extrinsic evidence is not admissible to add to, vary, or subtract from or contradict the terms of the written instrument. Where a doubt arises as to the true sense and meaning of the words themselves or there is any difficulty as to their application in the circumstances, then the sense and meaning of the words used in the written document may be investigated and determined by *viva voce* and documentary evidence outside of the instrument in dispute.

Can Parol Evidence be used to establish the presence of ambiguity?

McGillivray J.A. delivering the judgment for the Ontario Court of Appeal stated in *Alampi v. Swartz*, [1964] 1 O.R. 488 at 494, that extrinsic evidence could not be used to establish latent ambiguity. The ambiguity must be apparent and then the court will allow the use of extrinsic evidence. This proposition has been followed most recently in *Paragon Farms Ltd. v. H.D. Linn Development Services Inc.*, [1988] 6 W.W.R. 417 (Sask. Q.B.). However, the Ontario Court of Appeal appears to have taken a much more flexible approach in *TransCanada Pipelines, supra* at 298:

> The extrinsic evidence is admitted to assist the court to determine if there is in fact a latent ambiguity in the written document and, if there is, to ascertain how that ambiguity should be resolved. If, at a later stage, another court determines that the written document can be interpreted without regard to extrinsic evidence, no harm can have been done by its admission.

The *TransCanada Pipelines* decision is the more recent decision but *Alampi* continues to be widely cited for the opposite proposition. The *TransCanada* decision seems to set the threshold for admission of parol evidence too low, given the nature of the parol evidence rule. *Alampi* has been widely followed and is more in keeping with the spirit of the parol evidence rule.

What constitutes ambiguity?

Difficulties of interpretation do not amount to ambiguity and extrinsic evidence will not be allowed to resolve such difficulties [*St. Lawrence Petroleum v. Bailey Selburn Oil & Gas Ltd.* (1963), 41 D.L.R. (2d) 316 at 321 (S.C.C.), per Martland J. for the court].

The *Contra Proferentum* Doctrine

If there is ambiguity in a contract, it is interpreted against the author. Le Dain J. stated for the court in *Hillis Oil & Sales Ltd. v. Wynn's Can. Ltd.* (1986) 25 D.L.R. (4th) 649 at 657 (S.C.C.):

> The rule is, however, one of general application whenever, as in the case at bar, there is ambiguity in the meaning of a contract which one of the parties as the author of the document offers to the other, with no opportunity to modify its wording. The rule is stated in its general terms in *Anson's Law of Contract*, 25th ed. (1979), p. 151 as follows:
>
> > 'The words of written documents are construed more forcibly against the party using them. The rule is based on the principle that a man is responsible for ambiguities in his own expression, and has no right to induce another to contract with him on the supposition that his words mean one thing, while he hopes the Court will adopt a construction by which they would mean another thing, more to his advantage.'
>
> The rule is also stated in general terms by Estey J. in *McClelland & Stewart, supra,* at pp. 266-7 D.L.R., pp. 15-6 S.C.R., as follows:
>
> > 'That principle of interpretation applies to contracts and other documents on the simple theory that any ambiguity in a term of a contract must be resolved against the author if the choice is between him and the other party to the contract who did not participate in the drafting.'

In order to apply the doctrine both ambiguity and a one-sided contract are necessary.

ANALYSIS

Parol Evidence

A precondition to the admission of parol evidence is ambiguity. The $15,000 reference in paragraph 8 of the agreement can be construed as setting out the minimum bonus to which our client is entitled or as a second reference to the $15,000 dollar sum mentioned in paragraph 3. There is nothing in the agreement to resolve these conflicting interpretations. Accordingly, ambiguity is present and we should be allowed to introduce parol evidence.

Contra Proferentum

The *contra proferentum* doctrine requires ambiguity in a contract imposed by the party against whom the doctrine is used. The main weakness in our case is that the litigation centres on clauses that were themselves the result of last minute negotiations. This gives the contract the appearance of a freely negotiated agreement rather than a standard form imposed on our client. We would require admission of parol evidence to show that these terms were imposed by the employer, Brown, on our client, who lacked independent legal advice with respect to these changes. The doctrine of *contra proferentum* can be seen as a common law response to situations of inequality of bargaining power.

The employer is clearly the more powerful of the two parties. With our case depicted in this light, we can argue that we have satisfied the underlying principle of the doctrine. If we are successful then the court will interpret paragraph 8 against the employer's interests and in our favour.

CONCLUSION

We can satisfy the necessary preconditions for the admission of parol evidence. Such evidence alone should win the case for us. With respect to the use of the doctrine of *contra proferentum*, we have a viable argument but our case is not the clearest possible situation for the application of the doctrine.

LIST OF AUTHORITIES

1. Fridman, *The Law of Contract in Canada* 2nd ed. (Toronto: Carswell, 1986).
2. Waddams, *The Law of Contracts* 2nd ed. (Toronto: Canada Law Book, 1984).
3. The *Canadian Abridgment*
4. Noted Up Cases with *Canadian Case Citations* and performed a computer search.

Selective Topical Bibliography

This selective topical bibliography, on key substantive areas of law, is intended to save the researcher time by outlining some of the key topical law reports, looseleafs, treatises, and topical periodicals. When using the bibliography, if you do not see a heading corresponding to your topic area, consider checking under topic headings related to your topic area. The reader should be cautioned that the bibliography does not purport to be exhaustive. You should always check your law library to determine if there are any other sources relevant to your specific research problem. As elsewhere in the book, the emphasis is on Canadian material. Foreign material is only cited where there is a shortage of qualitative Canadian material, or where there is a well-known foreign text that is frequently cited and relied on in Canada.

ADMINISTRATIVE LAW

Topical Law Reports

Administrative Law Reports

Looseleaf Service

Macaulay, *Practice and Procedure Before Administrative Tribunals* (Toronto: Carswell, 1988)

Texts

Arrowsmith, *Government Procurement and Judicial Review* (Toronto: Carswell, 1988)
Blake, *Administrative Law in Canada* (Toronto: Butterworths, 1992)
Dussault & Borgeat, *Administrative Law: A Treatise*, 2nd ed. (Toronto: Carswell, 1986, 1989, 1990)
Holland & McGowan, *Delegated Legislation in Canada* (Toronto: Carswell, 1989)
Jones, *Garner's Administrative Law*, 7th ed. (London: Butterworths, 1989)
Jones & DeVillars, *Principles of Administrative Law* (Toronto: Carswell, 1985)
McFarlane, Pun & Loparco, *The Annotated Unemployment Insurance Act 1993* (Toronto: Carswell, 1992)

Moskoff *et al.*, *Administrative Tribunals: A Practice Handbook for Legal Counsel* (Aurora: Canada Law Book, 1989)

Topical Journals

Canadian Journal of Administrative Law and Practice

BANKING LAW

Topical Law Reports

Business Law Reports

Looseleaf Service

Sarna, *Letters of Credit: The Law and Current Practice*, 3rd ed. (Toronto: Carswell)
Youard, *International Financial Documentation* (Toronto: Butterworths)

Annotated Acts

David, *The Annotated Bank Act 1993* (Toronto: Carswell, 1993)
Manzer, *The Bank Act Annotated & Related Statutes* (Toronto: Butterworths)

Newsletter

Canadian Financial Services Alert

Texts

General

Baxter, *Law of Banking*, 4th ed. (Toronto: Carswell, 1992)
Crawford, *Crawford and Falconbridge Banking and Bills of Exchange*, 8th ed. (Aurora: Canada Law Book, 1988)
Geva & Greenwood, *Banking & Finance Law Review* (Toronto: Carswell)
Hapgood & Neate, *Paget: Law of Banking* (London: Butterworths, 1989)
Maddaugh, *Bank Act of Canada*, 5th ed. (Toronto: Carswell, 1992)
Ogilvie, *Canadian Banking Law* (Toronto: Carswell, 1991)

The Law of Guarantee

McGuinness, *The Law of Guarantee: A Treatise on Guarantee, Indemnity and the Standby Letter of Credit* (Co-published by Toronto: Carswell and London: Sweet & Maxwell, 1986)

International Finance

Baxter, *International Banking and Finance* (Toronto: Carswell, 1989)

Tennekoon, *The Law and Regulation of International Finance* (Toronto: Butterworths, 1992)

Sarwal, ed., *KPMG International Handbook of Financial Instruments and Transactions* (Toronto: Butterworths, 1989)

Topical Journals

Banking & Finance Law Review
National Banking Review
National Creditor/Debtor Review

BANKRUPTCY, INSOLVENCY AND DEBTOR-CREDITOR LAW

Topical Law Reports

Canadian Bankruptcy Reports (Toronto: Carswell)

Looseleaf Services

Fraser, *Debt Collection: A Step-by-Step Legal Guide* (Aurora: Canada Law Book)

Houlden & Morawetz, *Bankruptcy and Insolvency Law of Canada*, 3rd ed. (Toronto: Carswell)

Honsberger, *Debt Restructuring Principles and Practice* (Aurora: Canada Law Book)

Sarna, *Bankruptcy of Corporations* (Montreal: Jewel Publications)

Annotated Act

Houlden & Morawetz, *Annotated Bankruptcy and Insolvency Act 1993* (Toronto: Carswell, 1992)

Newsletter

Commercial Insolvency Reporter (Toronto: Butterworths)

Texts

Allen & Orvey, *International Insolvency* (Toronto: Butterworths, 1992)

Bennett, *Bennett on Collections* 1993 ed. (Toronto: Carswell, 1992)

Bennett, *Bennett on Creditors' and Debtors' Rights and Remedies*, 3rd ed. (Toronto: Carswell, 1992)

Bennett, *Receiverships* (Toronto: Carswell, 1985)

Dunlop, *Creditor-Debtor Law in Canada* (Toronto: Carswell, 1982 and 1986 supplement)

Gertner *et al.*, *Debtor and Creditor: Cases and Commentary* 3rd ed. (Toronto: Carswell, 1987)

Herdy, *Crown Priority in Insolvency* (Toronto: Carswell, 1986)

Leonard, *Guide to Commercial Insolvency in Canada* (Toronto: Butterworths, 1988)

Lingard, *Corporate Rescues and Insolvencies*, 2nd ed. (London: Butterworths, 1989)

Meehan & Vaartnou, *Creditors' Remedies in Alberta* (Toronto: Carswell, 1987)

Topical Journals

Canada

National Insolvency Review

American

American Bankruptcy Law Journal
Bankruptcy Developments Journal

CIVIL PROCEDURE

Topical Law Reports

Carswell's Practice Cases

Looseleaf Services

Rules and Legislation

Busby, *Manitoba Queen's Bench Rules Annotated* (Toronto: Carswell)

Chiasson, ed., *Annotations to the New Brunswick Rules of Court* (Toronto: Carswell)

Ehrlich, *Nova Scotia Annotated Rules of Practice* (Toronto: Carswell)

Gale *et al.*, *Holmested & Gale on the Judicature Act of Ontario & Rules of Practice* (Toronto: Carswell)

Hughes, *Federal Court of Canada Service* (Toronto: Butterworths)

Sgayias *et al.*, *Federal Court Practice 1993* (Toronto: Carswell, 1992)

Vogel, *Cohen Melnitzer's Civil Procedure in Practice* (Toronto: Carswell, 1989)

Watson & Perkins, *Holmested & Watson Ontario Civil Procedure* (Toronto: Carswell)

Limitation Periods

Alberta Limitations Manual (Toronto: Butterworths)

Crisp, Ditta & Joffe, *Federal Limitation Periods* (Markham: Butterworths, 1992)

Crisp, Ditta & Joffe, *Ontario Limitation Periods* (Markham: Butterworths, 1992)

Fainstein, Russel & Busby, *Manitoba Queen's Bench Act and Rules Annotated* (Winnipeg: Legal Research Institute of the University of Manitoba)

Nova Scotia Civil Procedure and Related Rules (Halifax: Queen's Printer)

Costs

Orkin, *The Law of Costs* (Aurora: Canada Law Book)

Drafting for Litigation

Carthy, Millar & Cowan, *The Ontario Annual Practice* (Aurora: Canada Law Book 1992)

Hayes, ed., *Williston & Rolls Court Forms*, 2nd ed. (Toronto: Butterworths)

McLachlin & Taylor, eds. (Irvine, Revising Editor), *British Columbia Court Forms* (Vancouver: Butterworths)

Practice

Fraser & Horn, *Conduct of Civil Litigation in British Columbia* (Toronto: Butterworths)

McLachlin & Taylor, *British Columbia Practice*, 2nd ed. (Toronto: Butterworths)

Tax

Slutsky, *Tax Aspects of Litigation* (Toronto: Carswell)

Discovery

Cudmore, *Cudmore, Choate on Discovery*, 2nd ed. (Toronto: Carswell, 1992)

Forms

Godin & Rouse, *New Brunswick Court Forms/Formulaire de procédure du Nouveau-Brunswick* (Toronto: Carswell)

Annotated Rules — Non-Looseleafs

Boock, Turriff & Dillon, *The British Columbia Annual Practice 1992* (Vancouver: Western Legal Publications (1982) Ltd.)

Watson & McGowan, *Ontario Civil Practice 1993* (Toronto: Carswell, 1992)

Texts

General

Sarna, *The Law of Declaratory Judgments*, 2nd ed. (Toronto: Carswell, 1988)

Stockwood, *Civil Litigation*, 3rd ed. (Toronto: Carswell, 1992)

Limitation Periods

Mew & Haberman, *The Law of Limitations (Toronto: Butterworths, 1991)*

Motions

Hendriks, *Court Motions Handbook* (Toronto: Carswell, 1991)

Practice

Brian & Brown, *Supreme Court of Canada Practice 1991-92* (Toronto: Carswell, 1991)

Zuker, *Ontario Small Claims Court Practice 1993* (Toronto: Carswell, 1992)

Tax

McMechan & Bourgard, *Tax Court Practice 1993* (Toronto: Carswell, 1992)

Topical Journals

Advocate's Quarterly

Digest Services

The Weekly Digest of Civil Procedure
Western Practice Digest 1992

COMPETITION LAW

Report Series

Business Law Reports

Looseleaf Services

Addy & Vanveen, *Competition Law Service* (Aurora: Canada Law Book)
Affleck & McCracken, *Canadian Competition Law* (Toronto: Carswell)
Kaiser, *Competition Law in Canada* (Toronto: Mathew Bender & Co. Inc.)

Annotated Act — New Volume Issued Yearly

Nozick & Neff, *The Annotated Competition Act 1992* (Toronto: Carswell, 1992)

Office Consolidation

The Competition Act and Regulations (Toronto: Butterworths, 1991)

Texts

Crampton, *Mergers and the Competition Act* (Toronto: Carswell, 1990)
Mungovan, *Competition Law: A Legal Handbook for Business* (Toronto: Butterworths, 1990)
Roberts, *Roberts on Competition/Antitrust: Canada and the United States*, 2nd ed. (Toronto: Butterworths, 1992)
Trebilcock, *The Common Law of Restraint of Trade: A Legal and Economic Analysis* (Toronto: Carswell, 1987)

COMPUTER LAW

Topical Law Reports

Canadian Computer Law Reporter

Looseleaf Services

Computer Law — General

CCH Guide to Computer Law
Sookman, *Computer Law: Acquiring and Protecting Information Technology* (Toronto: Carswell)

Computer Contracts

Bigelow, *Computer Contracts: Negotiating, Drafting* (New York: Mattney Bender & Co. Inc.)

Raysman & Brown, *Computer Law: Drafting and Negotiating Forms and Agreements* (New York: Law Journal Seminar Press)

Texts

Computer Law — General

Gemignani, *Computer Law* (Rochester, N.Y.: Lawyers Co-operative Publishing Co., 1985)

Hughes, *Essays on Computer Law* (Melbourne: Longman House, 1990)

Mandell, *Computers, Data Processing and the Law: Text & Cases* (New York: West Publishing Co., 1984)

Mann, *Computer Technology and the Law in Canada (Toronto: Carswell, 1987)*

Sookman, *Computer Law: Acquiring and Protecting Information Technology* (Toronto: Carswell, 1989)

Tapper, *Computer Law*, 3rd ed. (London: Longman House, 1983)

Computer Contracts

Morgan & Stedman, *Computer Contracts*, 2nd ed. (London: Longman Group Ltd. 1985)

Takach, *Contracting for Computers: A Practical Guide to Negotiating Effective Contracts for the Acquisition of Computer Systems & Related Services* (Toronto: McGraw-Hill Ryerson, 1989)

Pearson, *Computer Contracts: An International Guide to Agreements & Software Protection* (Toronto: Methuen Publications, 1984)

Topical Journals

United States

Computer Law Journal

CONFLICT OF LAWS (PRIVATE INTERNATIONAL LAW)

Texts

Canadian

Castel, *Canadian Conflict of Laws*, 2nd ed. & 1990 Cumulative Supplement
(Toronto: Butterworths, 1990)
Castel, *Introduction to Conflict of Laws*, 2nd ed. (Toronto: Butterworths,
1986)
Green, *International Law: A Canadian Perspective*, 2nd ed. (Toronto:
Carswell, 1988)
Morgan, *International Law and the Canadian Courts: Sovereign Immunity,
Criminal Jurisdiction, Aliens' Rights and Taxation Powers* (Toronto:
Carswell, 1990)

English

Cheshire and North's Private International Law, 11th. ed. (London: But-
terworths, 1987)
Dicey and Morris on the Conflict of Laws, 11th. ed. (London: Stevens &
Sons Limited, 1987)

Topical Journals

Canadian Yearbook of International Law

CONSTITUTIONAL LAW

Topical Law Reports

Charter of Rights and Freedoms

Canadian Rights Reporter
Charter of Rights Decisions

Looseleaf Services

Charter of Rights and Freedoms

Hogg, *Constitutional Law of Canada*, 3rd ed. (Toronto: Carswell)
Laskin *et al.*, eds., *Canadian Charter of Rights Annotated* (Aurora: Canada
Law Book)

McLeod, Takach, Morton & Segal, *The Canadian Charter of Rights: The Prosecution and Defence of Criminal and Other Statutory Offences* (Toronto: Carswell)

Stratas, *The Charter of Rights in Litigation* (Toronto: Canada Law Book)

Tarnopolsky, *Discrimination and the Law Including Equality Rights Under the Charter* (Don Mills: Richard De Boo Publishers)

Division of Powers

Hogg, *Constitutional Law of Canada*, 3rd ed. (Toronto: Carswell)

Texts

General

Monahan, *Politics and the Constitution: The Charter, Federalism and the Supreme Court of Canada* (Toronto: Carswell, 1987)

Strayer, *The Canadian Constitution and the Courts* (Toronto: Butterworths, 1988)

Swinton, *The Supreme Court and Canadian Federalism: The Laskin-Dickson Years* (Toronto: Carswell, 1990)

Charter of Rights and Freedoms

Bayefsky, *International Human Rights Law: Use In Canadian Charter of Rights and Freedoms Litigation* (Toronto: Butterworths, 1992)

Beaudoin & Ratushny, *The Canadian Charter of Rights and Freedoms*, 2nd ed. (Toronto: Carswell, 1989)

Cooper-Stephenson, *Charter Damages Claims* (Toronto: Butterworths, 1990)

Fogarty, *Equality Rights and Their Limitations in the Charter* (Toronto: Carswell, 1987)

Gibson, *The Law of the Charter: Equality Rights* (Toronto: Carswell, 1990)

Finkelstein, MacLeod & Rogers, *Charter Issues in Civil Cases* (Toronto: Carswell, 1988)

McDonald, *Legal Rights in the Canadian Charter of Rights and Freedoms* 2nd ed. (Toronto: Carswell, 1987)

Salhany, *The Origin of Rights* (Toronto: Carswell)

Sharpe, ed., *Charter Litigation* (Toronto: Butterworths, 1986)

Schneiderman, *Freedom of Expression and the Charter* (Toronto: Carswell, 1991)

Trackman, *Reasoning with the Charter* (Toronto: Butterworths, 1991)

Division of Powers

Beatty, *The Canadian Production Constitutional Review: Talking Heads and the Supremes* (Toronto: Carswell, 1990)

Finkelstein, *Laskin's Canadian Constitutional Law*, 5th ed. (Toronto: Carswell, 1986)

Whitley, *Criminal Justice and the Constitution* (Toronto: Carswell, 1989)

American Constitutional Law

Tribe, *American Constitutional Law*, 2nd ed. (New York: The Foundation Press, Inc., 1988)

Topical Journals

National Journal of Constitutional Law

CONTRACT LAW

Looseleaf Services

General

CCH, *Canadian Commercial Law Guide*

Building Contracts

Goldsmith on Canadian Building Contracts, 4th ed. (Toronto: Carswell)

Computer Contracts

Bigelow, *Computer Contracts: Negotiations, Drafting* (New York: Matthey Bender & Co. Inc.)

Employment Contracts

Kutten & Reams, *Executive and Professional Employment Contracts* (New Hampshire: Butterworth Legal Publishers)

Saxe & Elliott, *Employment Contracts Handbook* (Aurora: Canada Law Book)

Damages

Pitch & Snyder, *Damages for Breach of Contract* (Toronto: Carswell)

Liens

Coulson, *Guide to Builders' Liens in British Columbia* (Toronto: Carswell)
Macklem & Bristow, *Construction, Builders' and Mechanics' Liens in Canada*, 6th ed. (Toronto: Carswell)

Texts

General

Boyle & Percy, *Contracts: Cases and Commentaries*, 4th ed. (Toronto: Carswell, 1989)
Furmston & Simpson, *Cheshire, Fifoot and Furmston's Law of Contracts*, 12th ed. (London: Butterworths, 1991)
Fridman, *The Law of Contract in Canada*, 2nd ed. (Toronto: Carswell, 1986)
Lake & Draetta, *Letters of Intend and other Precontractual Documents: Comparative Analysis & Forms* (Toronto: Butterworths, 1990)
Waddams, *The Law of Contracts* (Toronto: Canada Law Book, 1984)
Enforcement
Yorio, *Contract Enforcement: Specific Performance & Injunctions* (Boston: Little, Brown & Co., 1989)

Sale of Goods

Bridge, *Sale of Goods* (Toronto: Butterworths, 1984)
Fridman, *Sale of Goods in Canada* (Toronto: Carswell, 1986)

Law Reports

Construction Law Reports

CORPORATE LAW

Topical Law Reports

Business Law Reports
Canada Corporations Law Reporter
Personal Property Security Act Cases

Looseleaf Services

Manuals

Alberta Corporation Manual (Toronto: Carswell)
British Columbia Corporation Manual (Toronto: Carswell)

Canada Corporation Manual (Toronto: Carswell)
Commercial Transactions (Toronto: Butterworths)
O'Brien's Encyclopedia of Forms — Corporations Division II (Toronto: Canada Law Book)
Ontario Corporation Manual (Toronto: Carswell)
Quebec Corporation Manual (Toronto: Carswell)

General

Burke-Robertson & Drache, *Non-Share Capital Corporations* (Toronto: Carswell)
Davies, Ward & Beck, *Canadian Corporation Precedents*, 3rd ed. (Toronto: Carswell)
Davies, Ward & Beck, *Canadian Securities Law Precedents* (Toronto: Carswell)
Honsberger, ed., *O'Brien's Encyclopedia of Forms — Commercial and General Division 1* (Aurora: Canada Law Book)
Krishna, *Canadian Corporate Law Reporter* (Toronto: Butterworths)
Rossiter, *Business Legal Adviser* (Toronto: Carswell)
Taschereau, *Regulation of Financial Institutions* (Toronto: Carswell)
Zaid, *Canadian Franchise Guide* (Toronto: Carswell)

Annotated Business Corporations Acts

Adams, *Annotated Ontario Business Corporations Act* (Aurora: Canada Law Book)
Ames & Lettner, *Ontario Business Corporations Act, Annotated* (Toronto: Butterworths, 1990)
The Annotated Business Corporations Act of Alberta, 3rd ed. (Toronto: Carswell)
Annotated Canada Business Corporations Act (Montreal: Jewel Publications)
Cumberford, *The Annotated British Columbia Company Act*, 2nd ed. (Toronto: Carswell)
Thomas, *Canadian Business Corporations Act Annotated* (Toronto: Butterworths, 1992)

Limited Partnerships

Hepburn, *Limited Partnerships (Toronto: Carswell)*

Fiduciary Duties

Ellis, *Fiduciary Duties in Canada* (Toronto: Carswell)

Corporate Counsel

Canadian Corporate Counsel (Toronto: Emond Montgomery Publications Ltd.)

Texts

General

Clark, *Inequality of Bargaining Power: Judicial Intervention in Unconscionable and Improvident Bargains* (Toronto: Carswell, 1986)

Canada Business Corporations Act and Regulations, 12th ed. (Toronto: Carswell, 1992)

Day, *Ontario Corporate Procedures* (Toronto: Carswell, 1991)

Horsley *et al.*, *Fraser's Handbook on Canadian Company Law* (Toronto: Carswell, 1985)

Millard, *The Responsible Director* (Toronto: Carswell, 1989)

Ontario Business Corporations Act, Business Names Act and Regulations, 16th Ed. (Toronto: Carswell, 1992)

Ontario Securities Act and Regulations, 21st ed. (Toronto: Carswell, 1992)

Sarna, *Corporate Structure, Finance and Operations* (Toronto: Carswell)

Sutherland, *Fraser & Stewart: Company Law of Canada*, 6th ed. (Toronto: Carswell, 1993)

Waldron, *The Law of Interest in Canada* (Toronto: Carswell, 1992)

Wegenast, *The Law of Canadian Companies (1931)* (Toronto: Carswell, 1931 (reprinted 1980))

Welling, *Corporate Law in Canada the Governing Principles*, 2nd ed. (Toronto: Butterworths, 1991)

Corporate Counsel

Gunz, *The New Corporate Counsel* (Toronto: Carswell, 1991)

Free Trade

Goodman & Goodman, Johnson and Schachter *Free Trade Agreement: A Comprehensive Guide* (Aurora: Canada Law Book)

International Commercial Arbitration

Park & Cromie, *International Commercial Litigation* (Toronto: Butterworths, 1990)

Annotated Acts

Gray, *The Annotated Ontario Business Corporations Act 1993* (Toronto: Carswell, 1992)

Topical Journals

Canadian Business Law Journal
Canada-U.S. Business Law Review
Securities and Corporate Regulation Review

Newsletter

Business & the Law

CRIMINAL LAW

Topical Law Reports

Criminal

Canadian Criminal Cases
Canadian Criminal Injuries Compensation Board Decisions
Criminal Reports
Weekly Criminal Bulletin

Motor Vehicle Law

Motor Vehicle Reports

Looseleaf Services

General Criminal

Gibson, *Canadian Criminal Code Offences* (Toronto: Carswell)
Melnitzer, Dawson & Bentley, *The Defence Lawyers Trial Book* (Toronto: Butterworths)
Salhany, *Criminal Trial Handbook* (Toronto: Carswell, 1992)
Sinclair-Prowse & Bennett, *Working Manual of Criminal Law* (Toronto: Carswell)
Watt, *Criminal Law Precedents* (Toronto: Carswell)

Annotated Acts

Crankshaw's Criminal Code of Canada, R.S.C. 1985 (Toronto: Carswell)
Heather, *Snow's Annotated Criminal Code* (Toronto: Carswell)

Greenspan, *Martins' Criminal Code* (Aurora: Canada Law Book)

Evidence and Procedure

Balfour, *The Jury: A Handbook of Law and Procedure* (Toronto: Butterworths)

Ewaschuk, *Criminal Pleadings and Practice in Canada* (Aurora: Canada Law Book)

Gibson, *Criminal Law Evidence, Practice and Procedure* (Toronto: Carswell)

Hamilton, *Judicial Interim Release* (Toronto: Butterworths)

Kennedy, ed., *Aids to Jury Charges (Criminal)*, 2nd ed. (Aurora: Canada Law Book)

McWilliams, *Canadian Criminal Evidence*, 3rd ed. (Aurora: Canada Law Book)

Young Offenders

Platt, *Bala and Liles Young Offenders Service* (Toronto: Butterworths)

Harris, *Young Offenders Act Manual* (Aurora: Canada Law Book)

Driving Offences

Gold, *Drinking & Driving Law* (Toronto: Carswell)

Hamilton, *Impaired Driving and Breathalyzer Law* (Toronto: Butterworths)

McLeod *et al.*, *Breathalyzer Law in Canada: The Prosecution and Defence of Drinking and Driving Offences*, 3rd ed. (Toronto: Carswell)

McLeod *et al.*, *Criminal Code Driving Offences: A Companion Text for Breathalyzer Law in Canada* (Toronto: Carswell)

Segal, *Manual of Motor Vehicle Law*, 3rd Ed. (Toronto: Carswell)

Weapons Offences

Harris, *Weapons Offences Manual* (Aurora: Canada Law Book)

Charter

Atrens, *The Charter and Criminal Procedure* (Toronto: Butterworths)

McLeod *et al. The Canadian Charter of Rights* (Toronto: Carswell)

Hutchison & Morton, *Search and Seizure Law in Canada* (Toronto: Carswell)

Commercial Crime

Henderson, *Commercial Crime in Canada* (Toronto: Carswell)

Sentencing

Nadin-Davis, *Canadian Sentencing Digest* (Toronto: Carswell)

Prison Law

Conroy, *Canadian Prison Law* (Toronto: Butterworths)

Texts

General

Burrow, *A Practical Guide to Criminal Prosecutions* (Toronto: Carswell, 1992)

Colvin, *Principles of Criminal Law*, 2nd ed. (Toronto: Carswell, 1991)

Delisle & Stuart, *Learning Canadian Criminal Procedure*, 2nd ed. (Toronto: Carswell, 1991)

Friedland & Roach, *Criminal Law and Procedure Cases and Materials*, 6th ed. (Toronto: Emond, Montgomery Publications Limited, 1991)

Gold, *Annual Review of Criminal Law 1992* (Toronto: Carswell, 1992)

Heather, *Snow's Annotated Criminal Code*, Annual 1993 Bound ed. (Toronto: Carswell, 1992)

Knoll, *Criminal Law Defences* (Toronto: Carswell, 1987)

MacIntosh, *Fundamentals of the Criminal Justice System* (Toronto: Carswell, 1989)

Mewett & Manning, *Criminal Law*, 2nd ed. (Toronto: Butterworths, 1985)

Pink & Perrier, *From Crime to Punishment*, 2nd ed. (Toronto: Carswell, 1992)

Saunders & Mitchell, *Criminal Law in Context: An Introduction* (Toronto: Carswell, 1990)

Segal & Libman, *Annotated Rules of Criminal Practice 1992* (Toronto: Carswell, 1992)

Stuart & Delisle, *Learning Canadian Criminal Law*, 3rd ed. (Toronto: Carswell, 1990)

Stuart, *Canadian Criminal Law: A Treatise*, 2nd ed. (Toronto: Carswell, 1987)

Whitley, *Jurisdiction in Criminal Law* (Toronto: Carswell, 1989)

Evidence and Procedure

Chayko *et al.*, *Forensic Evidence in Canada* (Aurora: Canada Law Book, 1991)

Cox, *Criminal Evidence Handbook*, 2nd ed. (Aurora: Canada Law Book, 1991)

Fitzgerald, *The Guilty Plea and Summary Justice: A Guide for Practitioners* (Toronto: Carswell, 1990)

Gold, *Proceeds of Crime: A Manual with Commentary on Bill C-61* (Toronto: Carswell, 1989)

Granger *et al.*, *Canadian Criminal Jury Trials* (Toronto: Carswell, 1989)

Kaufman, *The Admissibility of Confessions* (Toronto: Carswell, 1979)

Levy, *The Examination of Witnesses in Criminal Cases*, 2nd ed. (Toronto: Carswell, 1991)

Martin, *Admissibility of Statements*, 7th. ed. (Aurora: Canada Law Book, 1989)

Mewett, *An Introduction to the Criminal Process in Canada*, 2nd ed. (Toronto: Carswell, 1992)

Rogers & Mitchell, *Mental Health Experts and the Criminal Courts* (Toronto: Carswell, 1991)

Salhany, *A Basic Guide to Evidence in Criminal Cases*, 2nd ed (Toronto: Carswell, 1992)

Salhany, *Canadian Criminal Procedure* (Aurora: Canada Law Book, 1989)

Stansfield, *Understanding Criminal Defences and Procedures* (Toronto: Carswell, 1992)

Stansfield, *Understanding Criminal Offences*, 3rd ed. (Toronto: Carswell, 1992)

Wells, *Eyewitness Identification* (Toronto: Carswell, 1988)

Charter

Finkelstein, *The Right to Counsel* (Toronto: Butterworths, 1988)

Morton & Hutchison, *The Presumption of Innocence* (Toronto: Carswell, 1987)

Paciocco, *Charter Principles and Proof in Criminal Cases* (Toronto: Carswell, 1987)

Stuart, *Charter Justice in Canadian Criminal Law* (Toronto: Carswell, 1991)

Whitley, *Criminal Justice and the Constitution* (Toronto: Carswell, 1989)

Offences Against Children

Harvey, *Sexual Offences Against Children* (Toronto: Butterworths, 1992)

McGuire & Grant, *Understanding Child Sexual Abuse* (Toronto: Butterworths)

Drug Offences

MacFarlane, *Drug Offences in Canada*, 2nd ed. (Aurora: Canada Law Book, 1986)

Provincial Offences

Ontario Provincial Offences, 1992 (Toronto: Carswell 1992)
Ontario Provincial Offences — Related Provincial Statutes 1992 (Toronto: Carswell, 1992)

Search and Seizure

Fontana, *The Law of Search and Seizure in Canada*, 3rd ed. (Toronto: Butterworths, 1992)

Sentencing

Code, *Trial Within a Reasonable Time* (Toronto: Carswell, 1992)
Cole & Manson, *Release from Imprisonment: The Law of Sentencing, Parole and Judicial Review* (Toronto: Carswell, 1990)
Ruby, *Sentencing*, 3rd ed. (Toronto: Butterworths, 1987)

Young Offenders

Platt, *Young Offenders Law in Canada* (Toronto: Butterworths, 1989)

Extradition Law

Warner, *La Forest's Extradition to and from Canada* (Aurora: Canada Law Book, 1991)

Jury Trials

Granger, Charron & Chumak, *Canadian Criminal Jury Trials* (Toronto: Carswell, 1989)

Inquests

Marshall, *Canadian Law of Inquests: A Handbook for Coroners, Medical Examiners, Counsel and Police*, 2nd ed. (Toronto: Carswell, 1991)

Police

Der & Kirkpatrick, *The Law of Firearms and Weapons* (Toronto: Carswell, 1989)
Hamilton & Shilton, *Annotated Police Services Act 1993* (Toronto: Carswell, 1992)
Jakob, *A Guide to Police Writing*, 2nd ed. (Toronto: Carswell, 1991)
Ramsay, *A Guide to Police Procedures* (Toronto: Carswell, 1992)
Rodrigues, *Police Officers Manual*, 12th ed. (Toronto: Carswell, 1991)

Salhany, *The Police Manual of Arrest, Seizure and Interrogation*, 5th ed. (Toronto: Carswell, 1991)

Woods, *Police Interrogation* (Toronto: Carswell, 1989)

Bail

Trotter, *The Law of Bail in Canada* (Toronto: Carswell, 1992)

Robbery

Libman, *The Law of Robbery* (Toronto: Carswell, 1990)

Topical Journals

Criminal Law Journal
Criminal Law Quarterly

Digests

Burbidge, *Digest of the Criminal Law of Canada* (Toronto: Carswell, 1980)
Criminal Law Digest, Revised Ed. (Toronto: Carswell)

Driving Offences

Hutchison & Marko, *The Law of Traffic Offences* (Toronto: Carswell, 1989)

Segal, *The Annotated Ontario Highway Traffic Act 1993* (Toronto, Carswell, 1992)

Segal & Libman, *Journal of Motor Vehicle Law* (Toronto: Carswell)

Segal, *Motor Vehicle Reports*, 2nd Series (Toronto: Carswell)

DAMAGES

Looseleaf Services

Berenblut & Rosen, *Litigation Accounting: the Quantification of Economic Damages* (Toronto: Carswell)

Hollander, *Managing Personal Injury Damages: A Lawyer's Guide* (Toronto: Carswell)

Personal Injury Damage Assessments in Alberta (Toronto: Butterworths)

Personal Injury Damage Assessments in British Columbia (Toronto: Butterworths)

Pitch & Snyder, *Damages for Breach of Contract*, 2nd ed. (Toronto: Carswell)

Goldsmith, *Damages for Personal Injury & Death in Canada* (Toronto: Carswell)

Waddams, *The Law of Damages*, 2nd ed. (Toronto: Canada Law Book)

Texts

General

Anderson, *Actuarial Evidence: Valuing Past and Future Income*, 2nd ed. (Toronto: Butterworths, 1986)

Bruce, *Assessment of Personal Injury Damages*, 2nd ed. (Toronto: Butterworths, 1992)

Charles, *Charles Handbook on Assessment of Damages in Personal Injury Cases*, 2nd ed. (Toronto: Carswell, 1990)

Cooper-Stephenson, *Charter Damages Claims* (Toronto: Carswell, 1990)

Feldthusen, *Economic Negligence: The Recovery of Pure Economic Loss*, 2nd ed. (Toronto: Butterworths, 1989)

Hogg, *Liability of the Crown*, 2nd ed. (Toronto: Carswell, 1989)

Lloyd & Ogilvie-Harris, *Personal Injury: A Medico-Legal Guide to Spine and Limbs* (Aurora: Canada Law Book, 1986)

Pitch & Snyder, *Damages for Breach of Contract* (Toronto: Carswell, 1989)

Remedies

Berryman, *Remedies: Issues and Perspectives* (Toronto: Carswell, 1991)

Fridman, *Restitution*, 2nd ed. (Toronto: Carswell, 1992)

Phillips, *Personal Remedies for Corporate Injuries* (Toronto: Carswell, 1992)

ENVIRONMENTAL LAW

Topical Law Reports

Canadian Environmental Law Reports, New Series

Looseleaf Services

General

Estrin, *Business Guide to Environmental Law* (Toronto: Carswell)

Franson & Lucas, *Canadian Environmental Law*, 2nd ed. (Toronto: Butterworths, 1992)

Garner, *Control of Pollution Encyclopedia* (London: Butterworths)

Roche & Sinclair, *Taxation of Canadian Mining Income* (Toronto: Carswell)

Environmental Assessment

Jeffrey, *Environmental Approvals in Canada: Procedure and Practice* (Toronto: Butterworths)

McCarthy Tétrault's Environmental Group, *McCarthy Tétrault Digest of Environmental Law and Environmental Assessment* (Toronto: Carswell)

Environmental Protection

Saxe, *Environmental Protection Act Annotated* (Aurora: Canada Law Book)

Energy & Oil and Gas Law

Canadian Institute of Resources Law, *Canada Energy Law Service — Alberta* (Toronto: Carswell)

Canadian Institute of Resources Law, *Canada Energy Law Service — Federal* (Toronto: Carswell)

Katchen & Bowhay, *Taxation of Canadian Oil & Gas Income* (Toronto: Carswell)

Verchere & Bankes, *Canadian Oil & Gas* (Toronto: Butterworths)

Texts

General

Estrin, *Environmental Law* (Toronto: Carswell, 1984)

Estrin, *Business Guide to Environmental Law* (Toronto: Carswell, 1992)

Muldoon, *Cross-Border Litigation: Environmental Rights and the Great Lakes Ecosystem* (Toronto: Carswell, 1987)

Poch, *Corporate and Municipal Environmental Law* (Toronto: Carswell, 1989)

Trading Canada's Natural Resources (Toronto: Carswell, 1987)

Dangerous Goods

Douma, *Transportation of Dangerous Goods in Canada* (Toronto: Butterworths, 1990)

Estrin, *Handle with Caution: Liability in the Production, Transportation and Disposal of Dangerous Substances* (Toronto: Carswell, 1986)

Energy Law

Canadian Institute of Resources Law, *Managing Natural Resources in a Federal State* (Toronto: Carswell, 1986)

Canadian Institute of Resources Law, *Trading Canada's Natural Resources* (Toronto: Carswell, 1986)

Lucas & Hunt, *Oil and Gas Law in Canada* (Toronto: Carswell, 1990)

Corporate Responsibility

Claydon, ed., *Corporate Environmental Responsibilities* (Toronto: Butterworths, 1991)

Saxe, *Environmental Offences: Corporate Responsibility and Executive Liability* (Aurora: Canada Law Book, 1990)

Topical Journals

Canada

Journal of Environmental Law and Practice

United States

Columbia Journal of Environmental Law
Harvard Environmental Law Review
Journal of Energy Natural Resources and Environmental Law
Journal of Environmental Law and Litigation
Pace Environmental Law Review
Stanford Environmental Law Journal
Temple Environmental Law and Technology Journal
Tulane Environmental Law Journal
UCLA Journal of Environmental Law and Policy
Villanova Environmental Law Journal
Virginia Environmental Law Journal

ESTATES, TRUSTS AND WILLS

Topical Law Reports

Canadian Estate Planning and Administration Reporter
Estates and Trusts Reports
Reports of Family Law

Annotated Acts

Schnurr, *The Annotated Ontario Estates Statutes 1993* (Toronto: Carswell, 1992)

Looseleaf Services

Estate Administration

Armstrong, *Estate Administration: A Solicitor's Reference Manual* (Toronto: Carswell)

C.C.H., *Canadian Estate Planning and Administration Reporter*

Lyons, ed. *British Columbia Probate and Estate Administration* (Vancouver: Continuing Legal Education Society of B.C.)

Trusts

Christopoulos & Kolinsky, *Taxation of Trusts and Beneficiaries* (Toronto: Carswell)

Janset, *Guide to Estate & Trust Accounting* (Toronto: Carswell)

Wills

Brule & MacGreg, eds., *O'Brien's Encyclopedia of Forms — Division V — Wills & Trusts* (Aurora: Canada Law Book)

Histrop & Cappon, *Will Precedents: A Solicitor's Manual* (Toronto: Carswell)

Scott-Harston & Johnson, *Tax Planned Will Precedents*, 3rd ed. (Toronto: Carswell)

Textbooks

Estate Litigation & Practice

Allen & Allen, *Estate Planning Handbook*, 2nd ed. (Toronto: Carswell, 1991)

Cullity & Brown, *Taxation and Estate Planning*, 3rd ed. (Toronto: Carswell, 1992)

Rintoul, *The Solicitor's Guide to Estate Practice in Ontario*, 2nd ed. (Toronto: Butterworths, 1990)

Rintoul, *Ontario Estate Administration* (Toronto: Butterworths, 1991)

Schnurr, *Estate Litigation* (Toronto: Carswell, 1987)

Probate Practice

Hull & Cullity, *MacDonnell, Sheard & Hull: Probate Practice*, 3rd ed. (Toronto: Carswell, 1981)

Trusts

Oosterhoff & Gillese, *Test, Commentary and Cases on Trusts*, 4th ed. (Toronto: Carswell, 1992)
Pettit, *Equity and the Law of Trusts*, 6th ed. (London: Butterworths, 1989)
Waters, *Law of Trusts in Canada*, 2nd ed. (Toronto: Carswell, 1984)

Wills

Feeney, *The Canadian of Law of Wills: Construction* (Toronto: Butterworths, 1987)
Feeney, *The Canadian Law of Wills: Probate* (Toronto: Butterworths, 1987)
McIntyre, *Practical Wills Drafting* (Toronto: Butterworths, 1992)
Oosterhoff, *Text, Commentary and Cases on Wills and Succession*, 3rd ed. (Toronto: Carswell, 1990)
Sheard, Hull and Fitzpatrick, *Canadian Forms of Wills*, 4th ed. (Toronto: Carswell, 1982)

Dependants

Amighetti, *The Law of Dependants' Relief in British Columbia* (Toronto: Carswell, 1991)

Topical Journals

Estates and Trusts Journal
Estates and Trusts Quarterly

EVIDENCE

Looseleaf Services

Cudmore, *Civil Evidence Handbook* (Toronto: Carswell)
Gibson, *Criminal Law Evidence: Practice and Procedure* (Toronto: Carswell)
Goldstein, *Visual Evidence: A Practitioner's Manual* (Toronto: Carswell)
Gorsky, Usprich & Brandt, *Evidence and Procedure in Canadian Labour Arbitration* (Toronto: Carswell)
McWilliams, *Canadian Criminal Evidence*, 3rd ed. (Aurora: Canada Law Book)
Mewett, *Witnesses* (Toronto: Carswell)

Annotated Acts

Beach, *The Annotated Canada Evidence Act and Related Provincial Statutes 1993* (Toronto: Carswell)

Texts

Anderson, *Actuarial Evidence: Valuing Past and Future Income*, 2nd ed. (Toronto: Carswell, 1986)

Brook, *A Lawyer's Guide to Probability and Statistics* (Toronto: Carswell, 1990)

Charles, Cromwell & Jabson, *Evidence and the Charter of Rights and Freedoms* (Toronto: Butterworths, 1989)

Cox, *Criminal Evidence Handbook*, 2nd ed. (Aurora: Canada Law Book, 1991)

Deutscher & Leonoff, *Identification Evidence* (Toronto: Carswell, 1991)

Jeffe, *A Guide to Pathological Evidence for Lawyers and Police Officers*, 3rd ed. (Toronto: Carswell, 1991)

Kenkel & Stephenson, *Forensic Evidence* (Toronto: Butterworths, 1992)

Sheppard, *Evidence* (Toronto: Carswell, 1989)

Sopinka, Lederman & Bryant, *The Law of Evidence in Canada* (1992)

Spencer & Flin, *The Evidence of Children: the Law and the Psychology* (London: Blackstone Press Ltd., 1990)

Tapper, ed., *Cross on Evidence*, 7th ed. (London: Butterworths, 1990)

Lectures

Applying the Law of Evidence: Tactics and Techniques for the Nineties (Toronto: Carswell, 1992)

FAMILY LAW

Topical Law Reports

Reports of Family Law, 3rd series

Looseleaf Services

General

CCH, *Family Law Guide*

Ferguson, ed., *Family Law Consolidated Statutes for Ontario, 1993* (Toronto: Carswell)

Ford, *The Ontario Annotated Family Law Service* (Toronto: Butterworths)

MacDonald, Weiler, Mesbur, Perkins & Wilton, *Law and Practice Under the Family Law Act of Ontario*, Revised ed. (Toronto: Carswell)

Divorce

MacDonald & Ferrier, *Canadian Divorce Law and Practice*, 2nd ed. (Toronto: Carswell)

Payne, *Payne's Divorce and Family Law Digest* (Toronto: Carswell)

Matrimonial Property, Support & Custody

Ferguson, *Matrimonial Property, Quantum & Custody Awards: A Practitioner's Guide to Pre-trial Settlement* (Toronto: Carswell)

Lewis & Mole, *Ontario Family Law Quantum Service* (Toronto: Butterworths)

McLeod & Mamo, *Matrimonial Property Law in Canada* (Toronto: Carswell)

Pensions

Pask, Haas & McComb, *Division of Pensions* (Toronto: Carswell)

Tax

Cole & Freedman, *Property Valuation and Income Tax Implications of Marital Dissolution* (Toronto: Carswell)

Rashkis & Benotto, *Income Tax and Family Law Handbook* (Toronto: Butterworths)

Domestic Contracts

Stark & MacLise, *Domestic Contracts* (Toronto: Carswell)

Cohabitation

Holland & Stalbecker-Pountney, eds., *Cohabitation: The Law in Canada* (Toronto: Carswell)

Practice & Precedents

British Columbia Family Practice Manual (Vancouver: the Continuing Legal Education Society of B.C.)

Cochrane, *Family Law in Ontario: A Practical Guide for Lawyers and Law Clerks* (Aurora: Canada Law Book)

Stewart, *Ontario — Family Law, Division VI, O'Brien's Encyclopedia of Forms* (Aurora: Canada Law Book)

Wilton & Miyauchi, *Enforcement of Family Law Orders and Agreements: Law and Practice* (Toronto: Carswell, 1989)

Child Protection

Bernstein, Paulseth, Ratcliffe & Scarcella, *Child Protection Law in Canada* (Toronto: Carswell)

Custody

McLeod, *Child Custody Law and Practice* (Toronto: Carswell)

Annotated Acts

Hainsworth, *Ontario Family Law Act Manual*, 2nd ed. (Aurora: Canada Law Book)

Hainsworth, *Reville's Divorce Act Annotated*, 3rd ed. (Aurora: Canada Law Book)

Korde, *British Columbia Family Law: Annotated Legislation* (Vancouver: Butterworths)

MacDonald & Wilton, *The Annotated Divorce Act 1993* (Toronto: Carswell, 1992)

MacDonald & Wilton, *The Annotated Family Law Act 1993* (Toronto: Carswell)

MacDonald & Wilton, *Annotated Ontario Family Law Act 1993* (Toronto: Carswell, 1992)

Texts

General

Family Law Consolidated Statutes for Ontario 1993 (Toronto: Carswell, 1992)

Freeman, ed., *The State, The Law and the Family* (London: Tavistock Publications, 1984)

Holman, Lyons, Hudson & Whiting, *Family Law Source Book for British Columbia* (Vancouver: The Continuing Legal Education Society of British Columbia, 1990)

Hovius, *Family Law: Cases, Notes and Materials*, 3rd ed. (Toronto: Carswell, 1992)

Hughes & Pask, *National Themes in Family Law* (Toronto: Carswell, 1988)

McLeod & Mamo, *Annual Review of Family Law 1992* (Toronto: Carswell)

Family Mediation

Irving & Benjamin, *Family Mediation: Theory and Practice of Dispute Resolution* (Toronto: Carswell, 1987)

Marriage Contracts

Roche & Simmonds, *Marriage Contracts* (Toronto: Carswell, 1988)

Property Rights

Hovius & Youdan, *The Law of Family Property* (Toronto: Carswell, 1991)
Payne, *Spousal Property Rights Under the Ontario Family Law Act* (Toronto: Butterworths, 1987)

Children's Rights

Canadian

Bala *et al.*, eds., *Canadian Child Welfare Law* (Toronto: Thompson Educational Publishing, 1991)
Landau, *Children's Rights in the Practice of Family Law* (Toronto: Carswell, 1986)
Phillips & Manning, *The Child and the Family Services Act* (Toronto: Butterworths, 1986)
Sammon, *Advocacy in Child Welfare Cases* (Toronto: Carswell, 1986)
Wilson & Tomlinson, *Wilson: Children and the Law* 2nd ed. (Toronto: Butterworths, 1986)

American

Duquette, *Advocation for the Child in Protection Proceedings* (Massachusetts: D.C. Heath & Company, 1990)

Religion in Family Law

Syrtash, *Religion and Family Law* (Toronto: Butterworths, 1992)
Syrtash, *Religion and Culture in Canadian Family Law* (Toronto: Butterworths, 1992)

Custody

Chisholm & MacNaughton, *Custody/Access Assessments: A Practical Guide for Lawyers and Assessors* (Toronto: Carswell, 1990)

Topical Journals

Canadian Journal of Family Law
Canadian Family Law Quarterly
Family Law Review

Newsletters

Money & Family Law

HEALTH LAW

Looseleafs

Marshall & Nakatsu, *Canadian Health Case Law Digest* (Toronto: Butterworths)

Dictionaries & Encyclopedias

Mason & McCall-Smith, *Medico-Legal Encyclopedia* (London: Butterworths, 1987)
Critchley, ed., *Butterworths Medical Dictionary*, 2nd ed. (London: Butterworths, 1980)

Texts

General

Rozovsky & Rozovsky, *Canadian Health Information: A Legal and Risk Management Guide*, 2nd ed. (Toronto: Butterworths, 1992)
Sharpe, *The Law and Medicine in Canada*, 2nd ed. (Toronto: Butterworths, 1987)
Sneiderman *et al.*, *Canadian Medical Law: An Introduction for Physicians and Other Health Care Professionals* (Toronto: Carswell, 1989)

Doctors

Emson, *The Doctor and the Law*, 2nd ed. (Toronto: Butterworths, 1989)
Meagher, Marr & Meagher, *Doctors and Hospitals: Legal Duties* (Toronto: Butterworths, 1991)
Picard, *Legal Liability of Doctors and Hospitals in Canada* (Toronto: Carswell, 1980)

Dentists

Rozovsky, *Canadian Dental Law* (Toronto: Butterworths, 1987)

Nurses

Morris, *Canadian Nurses and the Law* (Toronto: Butterworths)

Aids

Rozovsky & Rozovsky, *AIDS and Canadian Law* (Toronto: Butterworths, 1992)

Patient Records

Rozovsky & Rozovsky, *The Canadian Law of Patient Records* (Toronto: Butterworths, 1984)

Consent to Treatment

Rozovsky & Rozovsky, *The Canadian Law of Consent to Treatment* (Toronto: Butterworths, 1989)

Mental Health

Savage & McKague, *Mental Health Law in Canada* (Toronto: Butterworths, 1987)
Schneider, *Annotated Ontario Mental Health Statutes, 1993* (Toronto: Carswell)

Topical Journals

Health Law in Canada

IMMIGRATION AND REFUGEE LAW

Topical Law Reports

Immigration Appeal Cases
Immigration Law Reporter, 2nd series

Looseleaf Services

Grasnick, *Canada/U.S. Business Immigration Handbook* (Toronto: Carswell)
Waldman, *Immigration Law and Practice* (Toronto: Butterworths)

Annotated Statutes

Marrocco & Goslett, *The Annotated Immigration Act of Canada 1993* (Toronto: Carswell, 1992)

Marrocco, Goslett & Nigam, *The Annotated Citizenship Act 1993* (Toronto: Carswell, 1992)

Texts

Goodwin-Gill, *The Refugee in International Law* (Oxford: Clarendon Press, 1983)
Hathway, *The Law of Refugee Status* (Toronto: Butterworths, 1991)
Nash, ed., *Human Rights and the Protection of Refugees under International Law* (Halifax: Institute for Research on Public Policy, 1988)

Topical Journals

International Journal of Refugee Law

INJUNCTIONS

Texts

Walton, *Kerr on Injunctions*, 17th ed. (London: Sweet & Maxwell, 1989)
Sharpe, *Injunctions and Specific Performance* (Toronto: Canada Law Book, 1983)
Stockwood, *Injunctions: A Practical Handbook* (Toronto: Carswell, 1985)

INSURANCE LAW

Topical Law Reports

Canadian Cases on the Law of Insurance
Canadian Insurance Law Reporter

Looseleaf Services

General

The Canadian Insurance Law Service (Toronto: Stone & Cox Limited)
Insurance Case Law Digest (Toronto: Butterworths)

Health Insurance

The Canadian Insurance Law Service — Health (Toronto: Stone & Cox Limited)

Annotated Insurance Acts

Gregory & Gregory, *The Annotated British Columbia Insuance (Motor Vehicle Act)*, 2nd ed. (Toronto: Carswell)

Weir, *Annotated Insurance Act of Ontario* (Toronto: Carswell)

Fire

Hewitt & Reynolds, *Fire and Emergency Services Law in Canada* (Toronto: Carswell)

Annotated Act

Winsor & Radomski, *The Insurance Act of Ontario Annotated* (Toronto: Butterworths)

Encyclopedia

American

Bander & Bander, *Appleman's Insurance Law and Practice* (St. Paul: West Publishing Co., 1987)

Texts

General

Baer & Rendall, *Canadian Cases on the Law of Insurance*, 2nd Series (Toronto: Carswell)

Baer & Randall, *Cases on the Canadian Law of Insurance*, 4th ed. (Toronto: Carswell, 1988)

Brown & Menezes, *Insurance Law in Canada*, 2nd ed. (Toronto: Carswell, 1991)

Hodgin, *Legal Decisions Affecting Insurance* (London: Butterworths, 1992)

Norwood & Weir, *Norwood on Life Insurance Law in Canada* 2nd ed. (Toronto: Carswell, 1992)

Tierney & Braithwaite, *A Guide to Effective Insurance* (Toronto: Butterworths, 1992)

Automobile Insurance

Brown, *No-Fault Automobile Insurance in Canada* (Toronto: Carswell, 1988)

Newcombe, *The Standard Automobile Policy Annotated* (Toronto: Butterworths, 1986)

174 THE PRACTICAL GUIDE TO CANADIAN LEGAL RESEARCH

O'Donnell, *Automobile Insurance in Ontario* (Toronto: Butterworths, 1991)

General Liability

Hilliker, *Liability Insurance in Canada* (Toronto: Butterworths, 1991)
Sanderson, *The Comprehensive General Liability Policy: The Insurance Intent* (Toronto: Butterworths, 1990)

Topical Journals

Canadian

Canadian Insurance Law Review
Canadian Journal of Insurance Law

American

Tort & Insurance Law Journal

INTELLECTUAL PROPERTY LAW

Topical Law Reports

Canadian Intellectual Property Reports
Canadian Patent Reporter
Fox's Patent Cases — Canada

Digest Service

Digest of Canadian Intellectual Property Law (Toronto: Carswell)

Office Consolidations

The Copyright Act and Regulations (Toronto: Butterworths, 1990)
The Patent Act and Rules (Toronto: Butterworths, 1989)

Looseleaf Services

Copyright and Industrial Design

Hughes, *Hughes on Copyright and Industrial Design* (Toronto: Butterworths)
Richard, *Canadian Copyright Act — Annotated Robic-Leger* (Toronto: Carswell)

Sarna *et al., Annotated Copyright Act* (Montreal: Jewel Publications Limited)

Tamaro, *The Annotated Copyright Act 1992* (Toronto: Carswell, 1992)

Patents

Hughes *et al., Hughes and Woodley on Patents* (Toronto: Butterworths)

Trade-Marks

Robic-Leger, *Canadian Trade-Marks Act — Annotated* (Toronto: Carswell)

Topical Journals

Canadian Intellectual Property Review
Intellectual Property Journal

INTERNATIONAL LAW

Topical Law Reports

European Court Reports
International Law Reports
Law Reports of the Trials of War Criminals, 1947-49

Texts

General

Akehurst, *A Modern Introduction to International Law*, 6th ed. (London & Boston: Allen & Unwin, 1987)

Brierly, *The Law of Nations: An Introduction to the International Law of Peace*, 6th ed. (Oxford, Clarendon Press, 1963)

Brownlie, *Principles of Public International Law*, 3rd ed. (Oxford: Clarendon Press, 1979)

Carty, *The Decay of International Law: A Reappraisal of the Limits of Legal Imagination in International Affairs* (London: Manchester University Press, 1986)

Castel, *International Law, Chiefly as Interpreted and Applied in Canada*, 3rd ed. (Toronto: Butterworths, 1976)

Castel, *Extraterritoriality in International Trade: Canada and United States of America Practices Compared* (Toronto: Butterworths, 1988)

Green, *International Law: A Canadian Perspective*, 2nd ed. (Toronto: Carswell, 1989)

Kapoor & Kerr, *A Guide to Maritime Boundary Delimitations* (Toronto: Carswell, 1986)

McWhinney, *The International Court of Justice and the Western Tradition of International Law* (Dordrecht, the Netherlands: Martinus Nijhoff, 1987)

Morgan, *International Law and the Canadian Courts: Sovereign Immunity, Criminal Jurisdiction, Aliens' Rights and Taxation Powers* (Toronto: Carswell, 1990)

Prabhu, *The Annotated Customs Act 1992* (Toronto: Carswell, 1991)

Raworth, *Legal Guide to International Business Transactions* (Toronto: Carswell, 1991)

Rosenne, *Practice and Methods of International Law* (Dobbs Ferry, N.Y.: Oceana Publications, 1984)

European Communities

Adamson, *Free Movement and Establishment of Lawyers in Europe* (Toronto: Butterworths, 1992)

Butterworths Guide to the European Communities (London: Butterworths, 1989)

Deloitte, Haskins & Sells, *Deloitte's 1992 Guide* (London: Butterworths, 1989)

Trenton, ed., *Butterworths EC Brief* (London: Butterworths, 1990)

Vaughan, ed., *Law of European Communities Service* (Toronto: Butterworths, 1992)

GATT

Hudec, *The GATT Legal System and World Trade Diplomacy* 2nd ed. (Toronto: Butterworths/Co-published with Butterworths U.S.)

Japanese Law

Oda, *Modern Japanese Law* (London: Butterworths, 1989)

Free Trade

Gold & Leyton-Brown, *Trade-Offs on Free Trade: The Canada-U.S. Free Trade Agreement* (Toronto: Carswell, 1988)

Irish & Carasco, *The Legal Framework for Canada-United States Trade* (Toronto: Carswell, 1987)

Steger, McNairn *et al., A Concise Guide to the Canada-United States Free Trade Agreement* (Toronto: Carswell, 1988)

Topical Journals

Canada

Canadian Year Book of International Law

United States

American Journal of International Law
Brooklyn Journal of International Law
Harvard International Law Journal
Loyola of Los Angeles International and Comparative Law Journal
Michigan Journal of International Law
New York International Law Review
New York Law School Journal of International and Comparative Law
New York University Journal of International Law
Virginia Journal of International Law
Stanford Journal of International Law
Yale Journal of International Law

LABOUR AND EMPLOYMENT LAW

Report Series

Employment Law — General

Canadian Cases on Employment Law

Employment Benefits & Pensions

Canadian Employment Benefits and Pension Guide
Pension Review Board Reports

Human Rights

Canadian Human Rights Reporter
Ontario Human Rights Commission Reports

Labour Arbitration

Labour Arbitration Cases
British Columbia Decisions: Labour Arbitration

Labour Relations

Canadian Labour Law Cases

Canada Labour Relations Board Reports
British Columbia Labour Relations Board Decisions
Ontario Labour Relations Board Reports

Public Sector Labour Law

Public Service Staff Relations Board Decisions

Workers' Compensation

Workers' Compensation Appeals Tribunal Reporter

Looseleaf Services

General

CCH, *Canadian Employment and Equality Rights*
CCH, *Canadian Master Labour Guide*
Clarke, *Canada Labour Relations Board: Annotated Guide* (Aurora: Canada Law Book)
Sack & Winkler, *Labour Relations and Employment — Division VII, O'Brien's Encyclopedia of Forms* (Aurora: Canada Law Book)

Annotated Acts

Clarke, *Canada Labour Relations Board: An Annotated Guide* (Aurora: Canada Law Book)
Randazzo, *The Annotated Ontario Labour Relations Act 1993* (Toronto: Carswell)
Russell & DuMoulin, *British Columbia Annotated Industrial Relations Act* (Toronto: Butterworths)

Employment Benefits and Pensions

CCH., *Canadian Employment Benefits and Pension Guide*
McLarren, *Employment in Alberta: A Guide to Conditions of Work and Employee Benefits* (Toronto: Butterworths)
McLarren, *Employment in British Columbia: A Guide to Conditions of Work and Employee Benefits* (Toronto: Butterworths)
McLarren, *Employment in Ontario: A Guide to Conditions of Work and Employee Benefits* (Toronto: Butterworths)
Mercer, *The Mercer Pension Manual* (Toronto: Carswell)

Employment Standards

Parry, *Employment Standards Handbook* (Aurora: Canada Law Book)

Labour Arbitration

Brown & Beatty, *Canadian Labour Arbitration* (Aurora: Canada Law Book)

Gorsky, Usprich & Brandt, *Evidence and Procedure in Canadian Labour Arbitration* (Toronto: Carswell)

Willis, ed., *Canadian Labour Arbitration Summaries* (Aurora: Canada Law Book)

Occupational Health & Safety

CCH, *Canadian Employment Safety and Health Guide*

Ferguson, *WHMIS Compliance Manual* (Toronto: Carswell)

Humphrey & Edwards, *The Employer's Health & Safety Manual* (Scarborough: Thompson Professional Publishing)

Keith, *Ontario Health and Safety Law: A Comprehensive Guide* (Aurora: Canada Law Book)

Pay Equity

CCH, *Canadian Pay Equity Compliance Guide*

Wrongful Dismissal

Harris, *Wrongful Dismissal* (Toronto: Carswell)

Levitt, *Dismissal and Employment Law Digest* (Aurora: Canada Law Book)

Mole, *Wrongful Dismissal Practice Manual* (Toronto: Butterworths)

Sproat, *Employment Law Manual: Wrongful Dismissal, Human Rights and Employment Standards* (Toronto: Carswell)

Discrimination

Tarnopolsky, *Discrimination and the Law* (Toronto: Carswell)

Texts

General

Arthurs, Carter, Fudge & Glasbeek, *Labour Law and Industrial Relations in Canada*, 3rd ed. (Toronto: Butterworths, 1989)

Human Rights

Bowland, Nakatsu & O'Reilly, *The Annotated Ontario Human Rights Code 1993* (Toronto: Carswell, 1993)

Vizkelety, *Proving Discrimination in Canada* (Toronto: Carswell, 1987)

Employment Law

England, *Christie on Employment Law in Canada*, 2nd ed. (Toronto: Butterworths, 1992)

Grosman, *Federal Employment Law* (Toronto: Carswell, 1990)

Harris, *Canadian Cases on Employment Law* (Toronto: Carswell)

Ontario Employment and Labour Law (Toronto: Carswell, 1992)

Wrongful Dismissal

Audet & Bonhomme, *Wrongful Dismissal in Quebec* (Toronto: Butterworths/Co-published with Les Editions Yvon Blais, 1990)

Levitt, *The Law of Dismissal in Canada*, 2nd ed. (Aurora: Canada Law Book, 1992)

Mole, *The Wrongful Dismissal Handbook* (Toronto: Butterworths, 1990)

Collective Bargaining

Sanderson, *The Art of Collective Bargaining*, 2nd ed. (Aurora: Canada Law Book)

Labour Arbitration

Gunderson, Kaplan & Sack, *Labour Arbitration Yearbook*, 1991 (Toronto: Butterworths, 1991)

Palmer & Palmer, *Collective Agreement Arbitration in Canada*, 3rd ed. (Toronto: Butterworths, 1991)

Weatherill, *A Practical Guide to Labour Arbitration Procedure* (Aurora: Canada Law Book, 1987)

Labour Relations

Carrothers, Palmer & Rayner, *Collective Bargaining Law in Canada*, 2nd ed. (Toronto: Butterworths, 1986)

Dorsey, *Canada Labour Relations Board: Federal Law and Practice* (Toronto: Butterworths, 1986)

Foisy, Lavery & Martineau, *Canada Labour Relations Board Policies and Procedures* (Toronto: Carswell, 1983)

Sack & Mitchell, *Ontario Labour Relations Board Law and Practice* (1985)*
    *can be updated with *Ontario Labour Relations Board Law and Practice Citation Updater*

Snyder, *Annotated Canada Labour Code 1992* (Toronto: Carswell, 1992)

Occupational Health & Safety

Grossman, *The Law of Occupational Health & Safety in Ontario* (Toronto: Butterworths, 1988)

Humphrey & Edwards, *Canadian Occupational Health and Safety Cases* (Toronto: Carswell)

Sexual Harassment

Aggarwal, *Sexual Harassment in the Workplace* (Toronto: Butterworths, 1992)

Aggarwal, *Sexual Harassment: A Guide for Understanding and Prevention* (Toronto: Butterworths, 1992)

Pay Equity

Elliott, *Ontario's Equity Laws: A Complete Guide to Pay and Employment Equity* (Aurora: Canada Law Book)

Weiner & Gunderson, *Pay Equity: Issues, Options and Experiences* (Toronto: Butterworths, 1990)

Employment Equity

Lamarche, Courteau, eds., inc., *Les programmes d'accès à l'égalité en emploi* (Montreal, 1990)

Smoking, Alcohol, Drugs and the Workplace

Grossman & Price, *Tobacco Smoking and the Law in Canada* (Toronto: Butterworths, 1992)

Young, *Alcohol, Drugs and the Workplace* (Toronto: Butterworths, 1992)

Workers' Compensation

Dee, McCombie & Newhouse, *Worker's Compensation in Ontario* (Toronto: Butterworths, 1987)

Gilbert, *Workers' Compensation in Ontario: A Practical Guide to the Statute Policy and Procedures* (Aurora: Canada Law Book)

Ison, *Workers' Compensation in Canada* (Toronto: Butterworths, 1989)

Employment Contracts

Bowlby, Jarvis & Mole, *Employment Contracts: An Employer's Guide* (Toronto: Butterworths, 1991)

Topical Journals

Human Rights

Canadian Human Rights Advocate
Canadian Human Rights Yearbook

Labour Relations

Canadian Labour Law Journal
Industrial Relations

LANDLORD AND TENANT LAW

Looseleaf Service

Bentley, McNair & Butkus, *Williams & Rhodes Canadian Law of Landlord and Tenant*, 6th ed. (Toronto: Carswell)
Documani & Albert, *Ontario Residential Tenancies Law* (Toronto: Carswell)

Annotated Legislation

Butkus, *The Annotated Landlord & Tenant Act 1993* (Toronto: Carswell, 1992

Texts

Balfour, *Landlord and Tenant Law* (Toronto: Emond Montgomery, 1991)
Lamont, *Residential Tenancies*, 4th ed. (Toronto: Carswell, 1983)

MARINE LAW

Report Series

Lloyd's Law Reports

Texts

Buchan, *Mortgages of Chips: Marine Security in Canada* (Toronto: Butterworths, 1986)
Fernandes, *Marine Insurance Law of Canada* (Toronto: Butterworths, 1987)
Ivamy, *Marine Insurance*, 4th ed. (London: Butterworths, 1985)
Mocatta, Mustill, & Boyd, *Scrutton on Charterparties & Bills of Lading* (London: Sweet & Maxwell, 1984)

Norris, *The Law of Seamen*, 4th ed. (Rochester: The Lawyers Co-Operative Publishing Co., 1985)

Parks, *The Law and Practice of Marine Insurance and Average* (London: Stevens & Sons, 1988)

Tetley, *Marine Cargo Claims* (Toronto: Butterworths, 1989)

Tetley, *Maritime Liens and Claims* (Toronto: Butterworths, 1989)

Wilford, Coghlin & Kimball, *The Charters* (London: Lloyd's of London Press Ltd., 1989)

Wilson & Cooke, *Lowndes & Rudolf on the Law of General Average and the York-Antwerp Rules*, 11th ed. (London: Sweet & Maxwell, 1990)

Dictionaries

Ivamy, *Dictionary of Shipping Law* (London: Butterworths)

Topical Journal

Lloyd's Maritime & Commercial Law Quarterly

MUNICIPAL AND PLANNING LAW

Report Series

Land Compensation Reports
Municipal and Planning Law Reports, 2nd Series
Ontario Municipal Board Reports

Looseleaf Services

General

Doumani *et al.*, *MacFarlane and Macaulay on Land Use Planning, Practice, Procedure and Policy* (Toronto: Butterworths)

Macaulay & Doumani, *Ontario Land Development: Legislation and Practice* (Toronto: Carswell)

MacFarlane, *Land Use Planning: Practice, Procedure and Policy* (Toronto: Carswell)

Morgan, *The Digest of Municipal and Planning Law* (Toronto: Carswell)

Rogers, *Canadian Law of Planning and Zoning* (Toronto: Carswell)

Rogers, *The Law of Canadian Municipal Corporations*, 2nd ed. (Toronto: Carswell)

Weir & Foulds, *Ontario Planning Practice* (Aurora: Canada Law Book)

Expropriation

Coates & Waqué, *New Law of Expropriation* (Toronto: Carswell)

Annotated Acts

Auerback & James, *The Annotated Municipal Act of Ontario 1993* (Toronto: Carswell, 1992)
Weir & Foulds, *Ontario Planning Practice: Annotated Statutes and Regulations* (Aurora: Canada Law Book, 1989)

Texts

Boyd, *Expropriation in Canada: A Practitioner's Guide* (Aurora: Canada Law Book, 1988)
Laux, *Planning Law and Practice in Alberta* (Toronto: Carswell, 1989)
Makuch, *Canadian Municipal and Planning Law* (Toronto: Carswell, 1983)
Troister, *The Law of Subdivision Control* (Toronto: Carswell, 1988)

NATIVE LAW

Topical Law Reports

Canadian Native Law Cases
Canadian Native Law Reporter

Looseleaf Service

Reiter, *The Fundamental Principles of Indian Law* (Edmonton: First Nations Resource Council)
Woodward, *Native Law* (Toronto: Carswell)

Annotated Statute

Hawley, *The Annotated Indian Act 1993* (Toronto: Carswell, 1992)

Texts

Asch, *Hone and Native Land: Aboriginal Rights and the Canadian Constitution* (Toronto: Methuen, 1984)
Bartlett, *Indians and Taxation in Canada*, 2nd ed. (Regina: University of Saskatchewan Native Law Center, 1987)
Bartlett, *Aboriginal Water Rights in Canada: A Study of Aboriginal Title to Water and Indian Water Rights* (Calgary: Canadian Institute of Resources Law, 1986)

Boldt & Long, eds., *The Quest for Justice: Aboriginal Peoples and Aboriginal Rights* (Toronto: University of Toronto Press, 1985)

Clark, *Native Liberty, Crown Sovereignty* (Montreal & Kingston: McGill-Queen's University Press, 1991)

Clark, *Indian Title in Canada* (Toronto: Carswell, 1987)

Little Bear, Boldt & Long, eds., *Pathways to Self-Determination: Canadian Indians and the Canadian State* (Toronto: University of Toronto Press, 1984)

Moss, *History of Discriminatory Laws affecting Aboriginal People* (Ottawa: Library of Parliament Research Branch, 1987)

Reiter, *Indian Finance Law: Alternative Mechanisms and Strategies for Financing Reserve Public and Private Ventures* (Edmonton: First Nations Resource Council, 1991)

Reiter, *A Lega Guide to Conducting Business on Indian Reserves* (Edmonton: First Nations Resource Council, 1990)

Reiter, *An Examination of the Evolving Concept of Band Councils, their Authorities and Responsibilities, and their Statutory Instruments of Power* (Edmonton: First Nations Resource Council, 1990)

Ross, *Dancing With a Ghost: Exploring Indian Reality* (Toronto: Butterworths, 1992)

PERSONAL PROPERTY AND PERSONAL PROPERTY SECURITY LAW

Report Series

Personal Property Security Act Cases

Looseleaf Services

CCH, *Canadian Commercial Law Guide*

Goldberg & Golick, *Guide to Ontario Personal Property Security* (Toronto: Carswell)

McLaren, *Secured Transactions in Personal Property in Canada*, 2nd ed. (Toronto: Carswell)

Tay, *Law of Ontario Personal Property Security* (Toronto: Carswell)

Texts

Sale of Goods

Fridman, *Sale of Goods in Canada*, 3rd ed. (Toronto: Carswell, 1986)

Romero, *Sale of Goods* (Toronto: Carswell, 1986)

Alberta

Cuming & Wood, *Alberta Personal Property Security Act Handbook* (Toronto: Carswell, 1990)

Dixon, *Alberta Securities Act and Regulation Annotated 1993* (Toronto: Carswell, 1992)

British Columbia

Cuming & Wood, *British Columbia Personal Property Security Act Handbook* (Toronto: Carswell, 1990)

Read & Hempell, *British Columbia Securities Act and Regulation Annotated 1993* (Toronto: Carswell, 1992)

Saskatchewan

Cumming & Wood, *Handbook on the Saskatchewan Personal Property Security Act* (Law Reform Commission of Saskatchewan, 1987)

POVERTY LAW

Topical Law Reports

Social Assistance Review Board Decisions
Unemployment Insurance Commission Decisions of the Umpire

Texts

Banting, *The Welfare State and Canadian Federalism* (Ottawa: McGill-Queen's University Press, 1982)

Ismael, ed., *The Canadian Welfare State, Evolution and Transition* (Edmonton: University of Alberta Press, 1987)

Kairys, eds., *The Politics of Law* (New York: Pantheon Books, 1982)

Luban, *Lawyers and Justice: An Ethical Study* (Princeton: Princeton University Press, 1988)

McGilly, *Canada's Public Social Services* (Toronto: McClelland & Stewart, 1990)

Prosser, *Test Cases for the Poor: Legal Techniques in the Politics of Social Welfare* (London: Child Poverty Action Group, 1988)

Topical Journal

Journal of Law and Social Policy

RACISM AND THE LAW

Texts

Bell, *Race, Racism and American Law* (Boston: Little, Brown, 1980)
Cryderman, O'Toole, & Fleras, *Police, Race & Ethnicity*, 2nd ed. (Toronto: Butterworths, 1992)
Williams, *The Alchemy of Race and Rights* (Massachusetts: Harvard University Press, 1991)

Topical Journals

Canada

Canadian Human Rights Advocate
Canadian Human Rights Yearbook

United States

Columbia Human Rights Law Review
Harvard Human Rights Journal
Journal of Law and Inequality
New York Law School Journal of Human Rights

REAL ESTATE OR REAL PROPERTY LAW

Topical Law Reports

Real Property Reports, 2nd Series (Toronto: Carswell)

Looseleaf Services

General

Atlas, *Taxation of Real Estate in Canada* (Toronto: Carswell)
Campbell, *Canada Valuation Service* (Toronto: Carswell)
CCH, *British Columbia Real Estate Law Guide*
CCH, *Ontario Real Estate Law Guide*
DiCastri, *Registration of Title to Land* (Toronto: Carswell)
The Continuing Legal Education Society of British Columbia, *British Columbia Real Estate Practice Manual*
MacIntosh, *Nova Scotia Real Property Practice Manual* (Toronto: Butterworths)
McDermott *et al.*, *Canadian Commercial Real Estate Manual* (Toronto: Carswell)

Rosenblatt, *Digest of Real Property Law* (Toronto: Carswell)

Conveyancing

Di Castri, *The Law of Vendor and Purchaser*, 3rd ed. (Toronto: Carswell)
Di Castri, *Registration of Title to Land* (Toronto: Carswell)
Lamont, *Lamont on Real Estate Conveyancing* (Toronto: Carswell)

Residential Real Estate

Rice & McDougall, *Ontario Residential Real Estate Practice Manual* (Toronto: Butterworths)

Condominium Law

Loeb, *Condominium Law and Administration*, 2nd ed. (Toronto: Carswell)

Leases

Barker, *O'Brien's Encyclopedia of Forms — Division IV — Leases* (Aurora: Canada Law Book)

Mortgages

Dunn & Gray, *Marriott and Dunn: Practice in Mortgage Remedies in Ontario*, 5th ed. (Toronto: Carswell)
Lamont & Manning, *O'Brien's Encyclopedia of Forms — Division III — Conveyancing and Mortgages* (Aurora: Canada Law Book)

Texts

General

Burke, *Ontario Real Estate Procedures* (Toronto: Carswell, 1992)
Canadian Institute of Surveying and Mapping, *Survey Law in Canada* (Toronto: Carswell, 1989)
Donahue & Quinn, *Real Estate Practice in Ontario* (Toronto: Butterworths, 1990)
Foster, *Real Estate Agency Law* (Toronto: Carswell, 1984)
Oosterhoff & Rayner, *Anger & Honsberger, Law of Real Property*, 2nd ed. (Aurora: Canada Law Book, 1985)
Sinclair, *Introduction to Real Property Law* (Toronto: Butterworths, 1987)

Conveyancing

Kennedy, *Sterk's Alberta Conveyancing Law and Practice*, 2nd ed. (Toronto: Carswell, 1987)

Sharpe, *Conveyancing Requisitions* (Toronto: Butterworths, 1983)

Condominium Law

Baker, *Condominium Law in Ontario: A Practical Guide* (Aurora: Canada Law Book, 1991)

Leases

Haber, *Understanding the Commercial Agreement to Lease* (Aurora: Canada Law Book, 1990)

Mortgages

Price & Trussler, *Mortgage Actions in Alberta* (Toronto: Carswell, 1985)

Rayner & McLaren, *Falconbridge on Mortgages*, 4th ed. (Aurora: Canada Law Book, 1977)

Title Searching

Globe, *Title Searching in Ontario A Procedural Guide*, 3rd ed. (Toronto: Butterworths, 1991)

Haden, *Ontario Title Searching Handbook, 1993* (Toronto: Carswell, 1992)

Topical Journals

National Real Property Review

SECURITIES LAW

Report Series

Business Law Reports
Ontario Securities Commission Bulletin

Looseleaf Services

Alboini, *Securities Law and Practice* (Toronto: Carswell)

Davies, Ward & Beck, *Canadian Securities Law Precedents* (Toronto: Carswell)

Annually Updated and Reissued Volume

Stikeman, Elliot, *Legal for Life*, 4th ed. (Toronto: Carswell, 1992)

Texts

Gillen, *Securities Regulation in Canada* (Toronto: Carswell, 1992)

Topical Journals

Canadian

Canada-U.S. Business Law Review

American

Securities and Federal Corporate Law Report
Securities Law Review
Securities Regulation Law Journal

STATUTORY INTERPRETATION AND DRAFTING

Texts

Bennion, *Statutory Interpretation*, 2nd ed. (London: Butterworths, 1992)
Beaupré, *Interpreting Bilingual Legislation*, 2nd ed. (Toronto: Carswell, 1986)
Langan, *Maxwell on the Interpretation of Statutes* (London: Sweet & Maxwell, 1969)
Pigeon, *Drafting and Interpreting Legislation* (Toronto: Carswell, 1988)

TAX LAW

Topical Law Reports

Canada Tax Appeal Board Cases
Canada Tax Cases
Canada Customs and Excise Reports
Trade and Tariff Reports
CCH, Dominion Tax Cases

Looseleaf Services

General

CCH, *Canadian Tax Reporter*

Davies, Ward & Beck *et al., Ward's Tax Law and Planning* (Toronto: Carswell)

Drache, *Canada Tax Planning Service* (Toronto: Carswell)

Drache, *The Canadian Taxpayer* (Toronto: Carswell)

Hanson, *Canada Tax Manual* (Toronto: Carswell)

Renouf, *Canada Tax Cases Index and Citator* (Toronto: Carswell)

McNair, *Taxation of Farmers and Fishermen* (Toronto: Carswell)

Slutsky, *Tax Administration Reports* (Toronto: Carswell)

Slutsky, *Tax Regulations Reports* (Toronto: Carswell)

Stikeman, *Canada Tax Service* (Toronto: Carswell)

Stikeman, *Canada Tax Cases* (Toronto: Carswell)

Tax Research

Sherman, *Income Tax Research A Practical Guide* (Toronto: Carswell)

Provincial Tax

The Practitioner's Provincial Tax Services (Toronto: Carswell)

CCH, *Canadian Tax Objection & Appeal Procedures*

CCH, *Manitoba & Saskatchewan Tax Reporter*

CCH, *Maritimes Tax Reporter*

CCH, *Ontario Tax Reporter*

CCH, *Quebec Tax Reporter*

Income Tax

Canadian Income Tax Revised (Toronto: Butterworths)

CCH, *Access to Canadian Income Tax*

Cole & Freedman, *Property Valuation and Income Tax Implications of Marital Dissolution* (Toronto: Carswell)

MacDonald & Cronkwrighty *Income Taxation in Canada* (Toronto: Prentice-Hall)

Rashkis & Benotto, *Income Tax and Family Law Handbook* (Toronto: Butterworths)

Roche & Sinclair, *Taxation of Canadian Mining Income* (Toronto: Carswell)

Taxation of Charities and Trusts

Christopoulos & Kolinsky, *Taxation of Trusts and Beneficiaries* (Toronto: Carswell)

Drache, *Canadian Taxation of Charities and Donations* (Toronto: Carswell)

Commodity Tax

Thorne, Ernst & Whinney, *Commodity Tax Reports* (Toronto: De Boo's)

Goods and Services Tax

Albrecht, ed., *Butterworths Goods & Services Tax* (Toronto: Butterworths)
CCH, *Canadian Goods and Services Tax Reporter*
Sherman, *Canada GST Service* (Toronto: Carswell)
Taitz & Millar, *GST & Commodity Tax* (Toronto: Carswell)

Trade and Sales Tax

CCH, *Canada Sales Tax Reporter*

Text

Sherman, *Income Tax Act: Department of Finance Technical Notes*, 4th ed.
    Consolidated to 1992 (Toronto: Carswell, 1992)
Sherman, *The Practioner's Goods and Services Tax Annotated*, 2nd ed.
    (Toronto: Carswell, 1992)
Sherman, *Practitioner's Income Tax Act*, 3rd ed. (Toronto: Carswell, 1992)
Stikeman, *Stikeman Income Tax Act, Annotated*, 21st ed. (Toronto: Car-
    swell, 1992)
Stikeman, *Canada Trade & Sales Tax Cases* (Toronto: Carswell)

Taxation of Real Estate

CCH, *Canadian Real Estate Income Tax Guide*
Atlas, *Taxation of Real Estate in Canada* (Toronto: Carswell, 1989)

Topical Journal

Canadian Tax Journal

TORT LAW

Topical Law Reports

Canadian Cases on the Law of Torts

Looseleaf Service

Irvine, *Canadian Cases on the Law of Torts*, 2nd Series (Toronto: Carswell)
Klar, *Remedies in Tort* (Toronto: Carswell)
McBean, ed., *Remedies in Tort* (Toronto: Carswell)

Texts

General

Bird & Zauhar, *Recreation and the Law* (Toronto: Carswell, 1992)

Dias *et al*, eds., *Clerk and Lindsell on Torts* (London: Sweet & Maxwell, 1989)

Feldthusen, *Economic Negligence: The Recovery of Pure Economic Loss*, 2nd ed. (Toronto: Carswell, 1989)

Fleming, *The Law of Torts*, 7th ed. (Sydney: The Law Book Co., 1987)

Fridman, *The Law of Torts in Canada* (Toronto: Carswell, 1989)

Klar, *Tort Law* (Toronto: Carswell, 1991)

Linden, *Canadian Tort Law*, 4th ed. (Toronto: Butterworths, 1988)

Solomon & Feldthusen, *Cases and Materials on the Law of Torts*, 3rd ed. (Toronto: Carswell, 1991)

Defamation

Brown, *Law of Defamation* (Toronto: Carswell, 1987)

Libel and Slander

Carter-Ruck, *Carter-Ruck on Libel and Slander* (Toronto: Butterworths, 1992)

Gatley, *Gatley on Libel and Slander* (London: Sweet & Maxwell, 1981)

Porter, *Canadian Libel Practice* (Toronto: Butterworths, 1986)

Williams, *The Law of Libel and Slander in Canada* (Toronto: Butterworths, 1987)

WOMEN AND THE LAW

Looseleaf Services

Lefcourt, *Women and the Law* (New York: Clark Boardman Callaghan)

Texts

General

Brophy & Smart, *Women in Law* (London: Routledge & Kegan Paul, 1985)

Cornell, *Beyond Accommodation: Ethical Feminism, Deconstruction & the Law* (New York: Routledge, 1991)

Forer, *Unequal Protection: Women, Children and the Elderly in Court* (New York: W.W. Norton & Co., 1991)

Glendon, *Abortion and Divorce in Western Law* (Cambridge: Harvard University Press, 1987)

MacKinnon, *Feminism Unmodified: Discourses of Life and Law* (Cambridge: Harvard University Press, 1987)

Pask, ed., *Women, the Law and the Economy* (Toronto: Butterworths, 1985)

Razack, *Canadian Feminism and the Law* (Toronto: Second Story Press, 1991)

Rhode, *Justice and Gender* (Cambridge: Harvard University Press, 1989)

Smart, *Feminism and the Power of Law* (London: Routledge, 1989)

Tong, *Women, Sex, and the Law* (New Jersey: Rowman & Littlefield, 1984)

Sexual Assault

Boyle, *Sexual Assault* (Toronto: Carswell, 1984)

Gunn & Minch, *Sexual Assault: The Dilemma of Disclosure, the Question of Conviction* (Winnipeg: University of Manitoba, 1987)

Estrich, *Real Rape* (Cambridge: Harvard University Press, 1987)

Russell, *Rape in Marriage*, 2nd ed. (Bloomington, Minn: Indiana University Press, 1990)

Sexual Harassment

Sexual Harassment, *Aggarwal Harassment in the Workplace* (Toronto: Butterworths, 1992)

MacKinnon, *Sexual Harassment of Working Women: A Case of Sex Discrimination* (New Haven: Yale University Press, 1979)

Spousal Assault

Dutton, *The Domestic Assault of Women: Psychological and Criminal Justice Perspectives* (Boston: Allyn & Bacon Inc., 1988)

Ewing, *Battered Women Who Kill: Psychological Self-Self-Defence as Legal Justification* (Massachusetts: D.C. Health & Co., 1987)

Family Law

Busby *et al.*, eds., *Equality Issues in Family Law* (Winnipeg: Legal Research Institute of the University of Manitoba, 1990)

Chesler, *Mothers on Trial. The Battle for Children and Custody* (New York: McGraw-Hill Book Co., 1986)

Smart & Sevenhuijsen, eds., *Child Custody and the Politics of Gender* (London: Routledge, 1989)

Reproductive Rights

Feinman, ed., *The Criminalization of a Woman's Body* (New York: Harrington Park Press, 1992)

New Reproductive Technologies

Field, *Surrogate Motherhood: The Legal and Human Issues* (Maccachusetts: Harvard University Press, 1988)

Scutt, ed., *The Baby Machine — The Commercialisation of Motherhood* (Carlton, Australia: McCulloch Publishing, 1988)

Spallone & Steinberg, *Made to Order: The Myth of Reproductive and Genetic Progress* (New York: Pergamon Press, 1987)

Stanworth, ed., *Reproductive Technologies: Gender, Motherhood and Medicine* (Minneapolis: University of Minnesota Press, 1987)

Prostitution

Bell, ed., *Good Girls, Bad Girls: Sex Trade Workers and Feminists Face to Face* (Toronto: Women's Press, 1987)

Hobson, *Uneasy Virtue: The Politics of Prostitution and American Reform Tradition*, 2nd ed. (Chicago: University of Chicago Press, 1990)

Legal History

Backhouse, *Petticoats and Prejudice: Women and Law in Nineteenth Century Canada* (Toronto: Women's Press, for the Osgoode Society, 1991)

Topical Journals

Canada

Canadian Journal of Women and the Law

United States

Berkely Women's Law Journal
Columbia Journal of Gender and Law
Harvard Women's Law Journal
Women's Rights Law Reporter
Yale Journal of Law and Feminism

INDEX

A

Administrative tribunals, 6
American Digest System, 120
American Jurisprudence, 117
American Jurisprudence Proof of
    Facts, 117
Appellate Courts, 6, 7

B

Binding, law that is (as distinguished
    from persuasive), 3

C

Canadian Abridgment, chapter 11
    Canadian Law Online, 63-64
    definition, 55
    method, 58-63
    organization, 55-58
    Quick Reference Chart, 65
Canadian Abridgment Index to
    Canadian Legal Literature, 40
Canadian Encyclopedic Digest,
    chapter 4
    Canadian Abridgment, 35
    definition, 33
    method, 34-35
    organization, 33-34
    use, 33
Canadian Law Online, 63-64
Case Comments
    locating, 41
    writing, 129-130
Commerce Clearing House (C.C.H.)
    Looseleafs, 49-50
Common Law (defined), 5
Concurring Opinions (as
    distinguished from dissenting), 6
Conference and Seminar Materials,
    chapter 7
    definition, 44
    use, 44
    method, 44
Corpus Juris Secundum, 116
Constitution, 4
Constitutional Research, chapter 14
    federalism, 74-76

Charter

Charter of Rights and Freedoms,
    76-85
Court Structure, 7
    American, 115-116
    Canada, 7-8
    Chart — Canada, 12-19
    English, 109-110
Current Law Index, 40

D

Dissenting Opinions (as distinguished
    from concurring), 6

E

Encyclopedias
    American Jurisprudence, 117
    American Jurisprudence Proof of
        Facts, 117
    Canadian Encyclopedic Digest
        (C.E.D.), chapter 4
    Corpus Juris Secundum (West
        Publishing Company), 116
    Halsbury's, 110, 111, 114
Essays, 128-129

F

Foreign law, 7, 84

G

Gender Neutral Language, 128

H

Halsbury's, 110, 111, 114
Hansard, 82, 95

I

Index to Canadian Periodical
    Literature, 40
Index to Foreign Legal Periodicals, 40
Index to Legal Periodicals, 40
Index to Periodicals Related to Law,
    40-41
Industrial Periodicals, 105
Interpretation Acts, 94

J

Judicial Consideration (of statutes)
    61-63, 93
Jurisdiction, 6-7
    foreign law, 7

L

Law Reform Commission Reports,
    chapter 8, 83
    definition, 45
    use, 45
    method, 46
Law Reports, chapter 10
    Canada:
        definition, 51
            administrative tribunal reports,
                52
            cross-Canada reports, 51
            judicial origin reports, 51
            provincial reports, 52
            regional reports, 51-52
            topical reports, 52
        method, 53-54
        official (as distinguished from
            unofficial reports), 51
        organization, 52-53
        use, 53
    England, 111-112
    United States, 118, 119, 125-126
Legal Dictionaries, chapter 13, 119
    definition, 71
    use, 71
    sources, 71-72
Legal Journals Index, 40
Looseleaf Services, chapter 9
    Commerce Clearing House
        Looseleafs (C.C.H.) looseleafs,
        49-50
    definition, 47
    use, 48
    method, 48-49

M

Martindale-Hubbell Law Directory,
    106
Memoranda
    Databases, 104
    writing, 134
    sample legal memorandum, 135-140

N

Noting Up, 59-63
    Canada:
        Cases, 59-61
        Statutes, 61-63, 93-94
        Rules of Practice, 61-63
    England:
        Cases, 113
        Statutes, 114
    United States:
        Cases, 122
        Statutes, 123

P

Periodicals, chapter 6
    case comments, 41
    definition, 39
    indexes, 40-41
    use, 39
    method, 39-41
Persuasive, law that is (as
    distinguished from binding), 3
    decisions of administrative
        tribunals, 6
Press Reports, 105
Primary Sources of Law, 3-4
    constitution, 4
    judicial decisions, 5-6
    relative weight, 4
    regulations, 5
    statutes, 5
Prioritizing the Law, 9-10
    flow chart, 11

R

Regulations, 5, chapter 16
    Canada:
        research methods, 98-101
        updating, 98-101
            federal, 99
            British Columbia, 99
            Nova Scotia, 99
            Ontario, 100-101
    England, 114
Regulatory Interpretation, 101
Reports, see Law Reports
Research checklist, chapter 3
    contents, 23-27
    form, 28-31
    organization, 22

using checklist with flow chart for
  prioritizing the law, 22
Restatements of the Law, 118
Royal Commission Reports, 83

S

Secondary Sources of Law, 3
Social Science Research, 76, 83,
  104-105
Statutes, 5, chapter 15
  Canada:
    creation and amendments, 87-88
    research methods, 89-95
    tracing the history, 82, 94
    updating, 91-93
      federal, 91
      British Columbia, 91-92
      Nova Scotia, 92-93
      Ontario, 93
  England, 113-114
Statutory Interpretation, 93-95
Supreme Court Law Review, 41-42

T

Telephone Directories (government),
  103-104
Treatises, chapter 5
  Canadian Abridgment, 38
  definition, 37
  use, 37
  method, 37-38

U

Uniform Laws, 123-124
  Uniform Commercial Code, 7, 123
Unreported Decisions, chapter 12
  definition, 67
  method, 69-70
  sources, 67-68
  use, 67

W

Words and Phrases, 63, 71-72, 95,
  111, 119